APPALACHIAN HERITAGE

VOL. 44, NO. 2
SPRING 2016

ESTABLISHED IN 1973

PUBLISHED QUARTERLY
by Berea College
CPO 2166
205 N. Main Street
Berea, KY, 40404

www.appalachianheritage.net

 Periodicals postage paid at Berea, Kentucky, and at additional mailing offices. ISSN# 03632318.

Electronic submissions only at www.appalachianheritage.net

Distributed by the University of North Carolina Press. Basic subscription price: $30/year for individuals, $60/year for institutions. For subscription requests and inquiries, visit the magazine's website, email uncpress_journals@unc.edu, or call 919.962.4201.

CONTENTS

EDITOR'S NOTE

JASON HOWARD

I grew up in southeastern Kentucky near Straight Creek, a body of water with bends and curves that contradicted its name. My friends and I often waded in its placid waters, hunting for crawdads as the heat bugs sang a steady chorus in the brambles and treetops. But the creek was also prone to flooding. Each spring, heavy rains, erosion, and the effects of environmental industry conspired to create a rising, muddy tide that flooded fields, covered roadways, and threatened homes. In those times, the creek had a fury that stood in stark contrast to the gentle companion we knew in the summertime.

The changing moods and meanings of water appear often in Southern and Appalachian literature. Bestselling novelist Amy Greene, in her 2014 *tour de force Long Man*, writes of a river with a "damp slate smell, its eroding banks studded with oval rocks washed smooth as glass" that held power over the people living along its banks:

> *Like the Cherokees, Beulah thought the river might be speaking to her. She wondered...if it wasn't Long Man whispering to her about the people that lived along its shores, communicating in some way much older than hers, from before language. As close as the people of Yuneetah had lived to it, having fished from and drunk of and swam through its waters, maybe they too could have heard the truths it told if they'd listened closer.*

In this issue of *Appalachian Heritage*, a group of talented fiction writers—Mary Grimm, Tim Poland, and Jayne Moore Waldrop—have been listening intently to the waters that have haunted them and their characters. Their stories have been compiled in a Special Fiction Feature titled "Deep Waters," and each one reveals hidden fathoms of meaning found among the shoals, rapids, and dams.

As you read further, you will be submerged in the meditation of Susan Tekulve's essay "Silent Song" and the poetry of acclaimed writers including Rebecca Gayle Howell, Erik Reece, and Jeremy B. Jones. You will want to swim in the depths occupied by Crystal Wilkinson—who discusses her latest novel and offers great writing insight in her interview with novelist Silas House—and Stephanie Barton, who contributes a fascinating craft essay on silence in the work of memoirist Mary Karr and photographer Cindy Sherman.

Like Greene's character Beulah, you will want to listen to the truths in these pages. ■

GOING TO MOONVILLE

MARY GRIMM

In the car it was steamy, smoky. The heat on and off, the indows rolled up, then cracked, the smoke from Roger's cigarette flowing out in a thin stream. The stuffiness was the kind that made Evie carsick, the warm queasy air pressing on her. She could remember riding the bus to school and feeling just as she did now, that stale feeling in your stomach. The roads wound round and round, up and down hill, the fields beside them rising and falling until she had no idea where they were or what direction they were going. Moonville. I've been up there many times, Roger was saying. Used to go in high school, scare the girls, you know how it is.

Evie knew. Moonville. She didn't care so much if it was haunted or not. She didn't care about ghosts. What did they have to say that she wanted to hear? But she liked the sound of it, the idea of the moon. She liked the stories that went along with the ghosts—the lost town, the tunnel where the trains didn't run. She liked the past when it was a story, with people who were in love, not when it was history, dates listed in a book that would be on a test.

It's spooky up there, Roger said. Spooky but nice. He poked her, making her jump. I'll be there to protect you.

Evie laughed. She drank from her water bottle and opened the window again, letting her hand trail out on the side of the car, letting the wind chill her skin. It's getting cold, she said.

Roger put on the radio and started to sing along with Beyonce, acting silly, going off key on purpose, but Evie sighed. She was bored. It was spring again and she was still here, small town girl going nowhere. She'd started seeing Roger mainly because he was older. It was interesting that he was married. She'd seen his pale-skinned wife around, coming out of Kroger's with a bag of groceries, or at Pizza Crossing. He had a truck that she'd liked at first, but all he wanted to do was go offroad in it. When you've seen one mudhole, you've seen them all. Moonville. Why not? Bring on the ghosts, she said to Roger, and he echoed her, Bring them on, baby.

■ ■ ■

The sky was blue, feathered with clouds, the sun sinking through the layers. All of southeast Ohio was sunk in green, pocked and seamed with ravines, threaded with streams, gleam of waterfalls showing through the leafing trees. When the glaciers came the ice had gone only so far and no farther, leaving the land they touched smooth and rolling, ready for fields of corn and soybeans. But southeastern Ohio, un-iced, was rough and rocky, hard farming, tiny fields in pockets of bottom land, squeezed between the hills. Good for rockclimbers, for rollercoaster roads, good for getting lost, good for ghosts.

■ ■ ■

Can I have a juice box?

When we get there, OK?

When will we get there? Can I have ice cream?

There is no ice cream there. We're going to walk in the woods, remember? We're going to Moonville.

Moonville, Taylor said after her father. Moonville. The moon lives in Moonville, right?

Not really.

Then why is it Moonville?

I don't know, he said, in such a way that she was quiet for a while. Taylor could see the moon in the sky, pale like it always was in the daytime, like a white dish on a tablecloth. She could put her finger over it if she wanted to. She had the idea that it was bigger than it looked. As big as a car or a house. You could live in it, or someone could, a man. Or maybe he lived in Moonville. The car bounced and shook her. Her seatbelt lay loose in her lap, it had lost its tightness. The trees rushing by made her eyes hurt, but she kept them open, looking for cows or a dog. Back a ways there had been baby lambs, a hundred of them at least, falling down a green hill with their mammas running after them.

Are there baby lambs in Moonville, Taylor asked.

Maybe there used to be.

They had gone away, Taylor thought. She was named after someone on TV, a soap opera, and so was her sister who had gone away. Her sister Brooke. You can say a prayer to your sister Brooke, her sitter was always telling her. She can watch out for you from heaven. But she didn't believe this, because Brooke had been a tiny baby when she left and she couldn't even sit up by herself. Her mother had gone away too, but not to heaven.

Where did they go? she asked, but her father didn't answer. She hadn't expected him to. Her doll Laurette was in her lap and she spoke into Laurette's ear. Moonville, moonville, moonville.

■ ■ ■

"From the Lake Hope dam and State Route 278, turn onto Hope-Moonville Road, stay to the left at the fork. The third time you cross the old railroad bed, you are at the abandoned town of Moonville.... Pull off where the berm widens just past the bridge. Walk the old railroad bed to the left, cross Raccoon Creek and Moonville Tunnel will be 100 yards straight ahead. The tunnel is no longer visible from the road. Be careful crossing Raccoon Creek during times of high water." Visitor Information Brochure, Lake Hope State Park.

■ ■ ■

Irene hesitated on the bank. The water was rushing past her feet with a febrile intensity, brown and opaque, the foam dirty beige. Above the crossing rocks, it pooled deeply, the color of dark beer, tiny rafts of leaves floating serenely. The rocks themselves were damp and some of them were mossy.

She wanted to believe herself agile, lithe, someone who would think nothing of leaping from rock to rock, her hair flying behind her. But she had weak ankles and her back hurt. She felt the thickness around her middle, a weight that would hold her down. And her hair was too short now to fly. But—Moonville. It was on the other side, and she had to go. Caidin was already halfway across, his white fur wet to his shoulders. He looked back at her to see if she was coming. People told her he wasn't very smart, but they didn't know him, his sweetness, how he felt things. People being Ed, he ex-husband. He had never liked Caidin, not his name, not his color. German Shepherds weren't supposed to be white, he said.

She could feel the past like a spear through her body, its spent potency rising in her and falling away.

The air was full of sound and message. Timidly, she set her foot on the first rock, only a foot from the bank. It wobbled and she stepped the other foot quickly across, then stood there frozen. Caidin barked encouragement but her head was ringing, voices chiming one over the other. If only they said sensible things, she thought. Meaningless sounds, advertising jingles, lines of dialogue from sitcoms, things from the past. Since her operation they never shut up. Don't sit on cement or you'll get a chill down there and you'll never have babies—her mother's voice, cracked and foggy from cigarettes. Who needed to hear that? She was past worrying about babies. She had rechristened herself as an act of healing: Irene, her middle name, although everyone still called her Betty.

The next rock was a little farther away, she'd have to stretch. The water foamed around it with a sucking sound. Irene spent a little time watching a branch still bearing green leaves come down river past the gauntlet of the rocks. She had been here before, long ago, long ago. Moonville. Prom night. Voices from twenty-seven years ago still hung in the air. I dare you. I'll get my dress wet. Be careful of the beer. Her date had carried her across, her red lace gown dragging in the water, her hair streaming over his shoulder. She should have changed into shorts like some of the other girls. She could feel the past like a spear through her body, its spent potency rising in her and falling away. Bending her knees for more spring, she leaned toward the next rock.

■ ■ ■

In the forest the trees leaned toward each other, the wind rising a little. Green, they had to be green, their leaves had to grow toward the sun. Vines wove in the branches, May apple umbrellas shaded the moss. Things were buried in the ground: nuts, lost marbles, gum wrappers, small bones. Green the trees, silty brown the water.

■ ■ ■

Are we there?

We're almost there. Her father's hair was standing up at the back of his head which made him look like Mr. Jim's rooster who lived in a pine tree. Taylor was allowed to scatter his feed when she came through the hedge to visit. Mr. Jim used to work on the railroad, he had showed her his hat when he was the engineer. The rooster had another chicken for a friend and soon there would be chicks.

Laurette wants some juice, she said.

She'll have to wait for a goddamn minute.

You'll have to wait for a goddamn minute, Taylor said to Laurette, and her father laughed. Don't say that, he said. Don't listen to me.

There was nothing to look at, no houses, only the trees.

■ ■ ■

"At one time there were approximately 100 people living at Moonville. Moonville is thought to be named for a man called Moon who once operated a store in the town. Moonville is famous for two things: The Tunnel and the 'Moonville Ghost.'" Visitor Information Brochure, Lake Hope State Park.

■ ■ ■

Taylor put her hand on her father's thigh. He was wearing his old jeans and they were soft. She stroked it.

Don't do that baby girl. I'm driving.

Taylor made Laurette sit beside her, outside of the seatbelt. If there was an accident her head would hit the windshield and she would be dead, which meant gone. Laurette had hair the same color as Taylor, brown. Her body was hard plastic and her eyes opened and closed with a click. Her father had bought her at an auction for Taylor but she was as good as a new doll. Taylor closed Laurette's eyes with her finger and held them shut. She closed her own eyes. We're going to sleep, she said.

Taylor's father nodded his head. Go to sleep honey and we'll be there before you know it and then we'll have a picnic.

The picnic was juice boxes and Ritz crackers with American cheese and green olives and a Snickers bar to share and a bottle of beer for Taylor's father. They had packed it up in a bag from the Krogers. Got to get you out in the fresh air, her father had said. Get out of this poky old town, have a little fun. Taylor's father worked for the county which meant he got a dark tan. Taylor went to daycare or sometimes stayed with Aunt Amy who wasn't her aunt. Aunt Amy was fun except when she talked on the phone too much and then Taylor went out and played in her yard which wasn't the same as being out in the fresh air. Aunt Amy liked her father but he didn't like her as much. She talks too much, he told Taylor when she asked why not. He went out sometimes with a girl, but it wasn't anything serious. I'll be getting you a mamma sometime, he said to Taylor, but not just yet a while.

The car was slowing down, the car was stopping and Taylor stopped pretending to be asleep. Are we here? she said.

Almost, her father said. He took the bag and got out of the car and walked around to take Taylor's hand. There was nothing to see but more trees. Come on, he said and they started walking down a path which was just dirt. It's not far, he said. When Taylor looked back she could hardly see their car for all the green around it.

■ ■ ■

Why don't we just screw? Evie said. She'd gotten tired of the idea of Moonville.

That's in my plans. Roger was driving the car one-handed, and on each curve of the road Evie tensed as he went too close to the edge.

We want to go here, why? she said.

Just something to do, baby, someplace to be.

Someplace where they wouldn't run into his wife or someone who would tell her, as Evie knew. It was OK with her that he was married, but sometimes it was a pain. Why can't we go to Columbus, she said. We could stay in a motel and go out someplace.

There was no place in Logan to go, it was too small. No place she hadn't been before—five pizza places, a bookstore/ coffee shop, the Mexican restaurant, Jack's Steakhouse. These were the kinds of places you went, and she was tired of them.

If we drove to Columbus right now we could go out to dinner and then go and have sex and be back by midnight. Which was when Roger said his wife was expecting him.

Couldn't make it before one, if that. Roger pulled the car onto the edge of the road.

Is this it? Evie looked around. There's nothing here.

We have to walk in, Roger said, but he didn't open the door. He reached over and ran his hand down over her nearest breast.

I'm tired of doing it in cars.

Come on Evie, give me a kiss. He hooked his other hand around her neck and tugged her forward. Take your seatbelt off. He kissed her cheek and put his big tongue in her ear.

■■■

Caidin whined on the bank, wanting her to hurry across. Irene crouched, her bottom resting against her heels. The water rushed around her, its glassy little waves sucking at her rock, breaking into little rills and ruffles of foam. She was in the middle, she was glad to see. Midriver, midlife. She might live to be a hundred or more, after all, in spite of everything. Her Granny Staples had made it to a hundred and three, dried up like an apple left at the back of a cupboard. When she touched Irene it was like a twig scratching at her, a shudder at the back of her neck. Betty she'd been then, of course. Irene put her hand in the water. So cold. How white her hand looked under the water, greenish-white, wavering, unsolid, as if she might begin to dissolve and float away. The weather was strange. Not quite summer, but the season seemed already to be winding down, the heat weak and flavorless. Caidin barked sharply, looking into the woods, toward Moonville

What is it? she called. He was standing stiffly, his legs braced. He was sensitive, she thought. He knew what there was to know in heaven and on earth. Her ankles ached, and her knees were building up pain. She'd have to stand soon or she'd fall when she did. If she fell, she'd slide into the pool just below her. She imagined her face underwater, lit by the greenish light down there, just as if she were looking at herself in an old mirror. Lying there, the cold of the river rocks at your back, the water rushing past you, lie there and wait for what comes, wait for boredom if that's what comes, wait until you see your way.

How white her hand looked under the water, greenish-white, wavering, unsolid, as if she might begin to dissolve and float away.

Caidin, she called, and he turned to her. Caidin, she said again, using the weight of his glance to pull herself up. Now, she said to herself, facing the rocks.

■ ■ ■

Some say that the ghost is a conductor who fell on the track and was decapitated. Some say the ghost was a young man on his honeymoon who in his marital exuberance leaned too far out the train window. His head bounced back into the lap of his new bride, his blood staining her going-away dress. Some say the ghost was a man who worked for the railroad and lived in Moonville. He left a family party to go down and walk in front of the train, no one knew why, and now he walks down to the train every evening, as punctual as if he were punching a time clock, as if the train still ran. Some say that the ghost is many ghosts, the remains of the living people who worked and sang and ate in Moonville, who are buried in the little Moonville cemetery. They're restless, these ancient Moonville citizens, uneasy in their earth beds, getting up at all hours to dance as orbs of light that can be captured by the cameras of amateur ghost hunters.

■ ■ ■

Irene lay against the bank sobbing. Caidin put his head against her and licked her cheek. Her ankle hurt and she had a long scratch down her arm from where she'd grabbed at a thorn bush to stop herself from falling in. Her pants were wet to the thighs. The incision over her ribs ached and she put her hand on it to quiet it. Why is it so hard? she asked Caidin, who barked in answer. He barked again, and she said yes, yes, I made it across, I know. Caidin always looked on the bright side. She pulled herself up to the grassy verge and sat, legs crossed. To calm herself, she closed her eyes and let her mind roam, letting loose of her self.

■ ■ ■

I am lying in the grass, she said, and saw her hand against the sky as if she could push it back and unroll it. I am surrounded by the grass, a small forest, one with the ants and the grasshoppers. The sky stretched over her tightly, covering her, pressing her into the earth. She could feel her body quieting, relaxing into the hollows and lumps of the stream bank, just as the visualization tape had said.

Then the moon, which was silver and dusty. The craters were filled with a litter of rocks and sand, the ground gritty under her feet. Was it called the ground on the moon? or was that a word that could only be used on earth? Caidin whined in her ear, and she patted him, without opening her eyes. The sky looked black but she knew it was a blue so dark that no one could tell the difference. The stars were hung in it like a forest of earrings, each one sparkling. The sun a hard ball of light.

She opened her eyes to the river, letting its amber pools and white foam be beautiful again, unmenacing. She was on the other side. Now let's get up there, she said to Caidin. She wiped some mud from her hands, and then slapped her thigh, saying come on, come on boy. Above them the trestles loomed. The tracks had been taken away, and the trestles looked like Stonehenge, or so she preferred to think.

■ ■ ■

Evie could feel Roger shudder, and obligingly, she moaned and thrust her hips up. She'd come several minutes ago, neatly and quickly as she always did. She ran her hand down the back of his head, scratching his neck lightly with her fingernails, which he liked. Outside the car, she could see nothing but green, leaves and tree branches. A bird flew across the window and chirped. The feel of him sliding out of her was sort of nice, she thought, and she kissed the side of his head. He burrowed into the curve of her shoulder. Evie, Evie, he said. My God.

I think I hear somebody coming, she said. She wriggled out from under him and pulled her tank top down.

■ ■ ■

She'll be coming 'round the mountain when she comes, Taylor sang, her father chiming in. She'll be coming 'round the mountain she'll be coming 'round the mountain she'll be coming 'round the mountain when she comes. The path turned in circles, the trees marching by fast. That's a good old song, he said. Now where'd you learn that?

Aunt Amy taught me. She has it on a record.

Well, that's a good one.

Aunt Amy wanted to come, Taylor said.

Did she say that?

She said she'd make a picnic for us sometime.

She did, did she?

She said she'd make a pie.

Do you like Aunt Amy so much?

Taylor put her arms around Laurette and squeezed. She's OK, she said. I like pie.

Oh, everybody likes pie, don't you know? Everybody in the world or out of it, Taylor's father said. He sighed.

Brooke didn't like pie, Taylor said. She only liked milk. Don't you remember?

Her father didn't answer, and she squeezed Laurette harder, pushing her soft girl bones against Laurette's plastic. Laurette likes pie, she said, but her father still didn't say a thing.

■■■

This trail would have taken the Indians into prime hunting and wintering ground along Raccoon Creek.... I believe that this ancient "Buffalo Trace," as the old people in Vinton County named it to me, was abandoned after McArthurtown was established, c1815.... The trace down to the fording just above Moonville was very steep on both sides of Raccoon Creek. We know where the trail is on the north but haven't found it on the south side as it goes over the ridge and down to Pinney Hollow.
The Olde Forester

■■■

Here, yes and over there, they had built fires, they had danced. Irene picked up a rock from the circle of a fire ring. She stood just in front of the tunnel, letting the voices wash over her, her mother, her father, her brother, her girlfriends. All dead now or married. Teeny gone to Columbus, Diane a nurse with three children, Rosemary who had lived in a commune and then married twice, both times to a man with a limp. Come on, Betty, they called, I dare you, come on. Don't go in the dark with a boy, don't let me catch you. No one will have you if you don't keep yourself nice, you know what I mean.

Who wouldn't be a little crazy, she asked Caidin, who was standing quiet beside her, looking into the tunnel. But as everyone knew, if you could ask the question, you were all right.

Caidin licked her hand and they both looked into the tunnel. Its bricks were maybe a little darker than they had been the last time, very beautiful really, against the new green of the trees. She remembered the touch of a hand on her hand, her shoulder, her cheek, and she closed her eyes to make it more real, that time when her body was perfect, if only she had known it.

■■■

There were probably never many more than 100 residents, and almost all of them were exclusively miners and their families. There was a row of houses along the railroad tracks, a sawmill, schoolhouse, post office, general store, and a saloon. The last family left in 1947, by the 1960s all of the buildings were gone.... ohiotrespassers.com

■■■

Taylor was singing a new song, but only in her head. She sang it to Laurette, her mouth against Laurette's ear, but not moving her lips. We're going to Moonville, she sang, we're going to live in Moonville. Moonville is full of the moon. She was riding on her father's shoulders, bobbing up and down, all the landscape around her bobbing as he walked up the trail. She let her head bob even more so that her chin banged her chest.

What's going to be there? she asked. What will we see?

Just a tunnel, baby. There's a tunnel and a crick.

Can I go in the water?

We'll see.

Laurette can't go in the water. It'd wreck her innards.

Her father laughed. Maybe you can't either. It might be too cold.

It would wreck her innards, she thought, she'd be as cold as in the refrigerator. Cold as a mackerel, her grandmother said sometimes. A mackerel was a fish.

Will there be houses?

Not any more, her father said.

No lambs, no houses. They were gone. Taylor wriggled her toes in her shoes, getting ready to take them off for the crick, which was water, and not like a crick in the neck.

■ ■ ■

Her mother had been here, Irene knew, when she was young. Some of the letters were still sharp, the M, the E. But in the middle, the OO was softened, worn down. Her mother told stories about going there to picnic, crossing over the creek on the trestle. She said once she was there with her sister when the train still came through, and that they had heard it coming, but somehow ignored it or thought it was something else. The train came and they had to jump, but it was OK, for they were almost at the end of the trestle. If she hadn't been quick enough, there would have been no Irene, she'd said, laughing, although Irene couldn't see that it was funny.

No Irene, she said to Caidin, and then what would you do? You'd belong to Tom now. But then if she hadn't married Tom, would Tom have bought a dog that, as it turned out, he didn't like? Never mind, she told herself, the past was fixed, at least. You could count on it, no matter how horrible it might have been.

Her mother had said that they used to find bits of old teacups in Raccoon Creek, but that hadn't happened for a long time. Teacups from Moonville, plates, painted with violets and roses. Her mother had thrown them away, she said, another thing that Irene held against her, that she never kept things, that she had no sentiment.

She sat down where she could see both the tunnel and the creek.

■ ■ ■

The tunnel originally made by stone cutters from huge sandstone blocks. Refurbished with clay bricks in 1903-4. Tunnel about 30-40 ft high, 20-30 feet wide (across the bottom, close to 100 yards long). Some of the original sandstone can be seen at either end. The Moonville Ghost Web Ring

■ ■ ■

Roger was showing off, leaping up the trail, bounding out to scare Evie, howling like a dog. Who was the kid here, really. He said she was immature when she didn't want to have sex, or complained about not going out to a fancy place for dinner. If we love each other, those things don't matter, he said to her. Evie kept what she felt locked in her own head. She didn't think it was love. Love was joy, she thought, a desperate waiting, a falling together that went on and on. She hoped she'd kept her head straight about all that, no matter what she was doing with Roger.

Look here, Evie. Roger caught her arm and pulled her off the path.

What, she said. She pulled out her cigarettes and lit one.

It's a pawpaw tree. We used to have them on the farm.

We who? she said, meaning to be snotty. But he ignored her. You can shake them down from the trees when they're ripe.

Evie put her cigarette between her lips and took the tree in both hands, shaking as hard as she could. Far above her the thin limbs of the tree shimmied and rustled.

Not now, Roger said, they're not ripe now. There's nothing there until September maybe. They fall from the tree when they're ready.

Evie put her cigarette between her lips and took the tree in both hands, shaking as hard as she could.

But not now, Evie said. She drew sharply in on the cigarette before taking it out of her mouth. It was never now. Evie rolled her eyes. Whatever.

■ ■ ■

Taylor dabbled her fingers in the brown water. Her father was sitting on a rock, smoking, looking away, like he did sometimes. She sat Laurette down on the grass and started taking off her shoes. They pinched a little and she wriggled her toes in her socks, and then took off the socks. Laurette had shoes, too, and she took them off and set the 4 shoes in a row.

Now you see, Laurette, she said in a small breathy voice, you just put your feet in to see if it's cold. Laurette felt that it was cold, but Taylor was stern. You'll get used to it in a minute, see if you don't.

Laurette's skirt floated on the water like a flower. You'll see, it's going to be nice. Taylor edged toward the water, letting her toes feel the surface. The crick was running along fast and bubbly, leaves floating like little boats. She stretched her legs and inched forward.

Irene's knees hurt, and she felt that one of her headaches might be starting, but the grass was soft under her. She watched the welcoming dark of the tunnel entrance, thinking of old times. A bonfire, the passing of a bottle, the search for a soft spot. Her young body bent under someone's mouth. Her mother's face in those years, boxed and prim. Irene's belief in herself (although she was Betty then), her conviction that nothing could hurt her. Her hair had been long and pale brown, never dyed (for her mother wouldn't allow it), but now she saw that it had been as nice a color as blonde in its way. She had cut it for the wedding, as if it were a requirement for marriage to Tom, a stiffly sprayed bouffant like a helmet. Caidin was running toward her now, barking and she got onto her knees, pushing against the ground to raise herself up. Was he hurt? Someone was chasing him, and Irene's heart twisted in her chest.

There it is. Roger waved his hand like a magician, and in spite of herself, Evie felt eager, light, as if a curtain would draw back and reveal something she'd been dreaming of since she was a little girl. She'd been a dopy kid, she knew now, always wanting to be a ballerina or some shit like that. Ahead she could see something dark rising above and behind the trees, and she began to run.

Wait now, Roger called. She could hear him lumbering behind her but she didn't stop, she ran all out like she used to when she was ten. He sounded angry but he was old and he couldn't catch her, he'd have to stop and get his breath or he'd probably have a heart attack. She broke through the trees and there it was, the stone walls dark against the sky. A white dog was coming out of the dark mouth of the tunnel like a bullet, and a woman was crying out. Evie laughed, for it was so much better than she'd expected, the noise, the light and darkness, the drama. The dog ran toward her and she opened her arms to it.

Sound travels well in the tunnel. When a person whispers from one end of the tunnel, it can be heard all the way at the other side. Visitor Information Brochure, Lake Hope State Park.

Taylor's feet were wet, which was bad. You'll catch your death Aunt Amy said when she stepped in a puddle. Taylor could hear someone yelling. Her father looked up and then stood. Don't worry, she told Laurette. Her father was looking the other way, and she pushed Laurette into the water. You're drowning but don't worry, she said. To save her she had to get all the way in.

■ ■ ■

"The ghost of Moonville, after an absence of one year, has returned and is again at its old pranks, haunting B&O S-W freight trains and their crews. It appeared Monday night in front of fast freight No. 99 west bound, just east of the cut which is one half mile the other side of Moonville at the point where Engineer Lawhead lost his life and Engineer Walters was injured. The ghost, attired in a pure white robe, carried a lantern. It had a flowing white beard, its eyes glistened like balls of fire and surrounding it was a halo of twinkling stars. When the train stopped, the ghost stepped off the track and disappeared into the rocks nearby." The Chillicothe Gazette, 1895

■ ■ ■

Irene panted, trying to catch her breath. A young girl was holding Caidin, he was licking her face, and she was laughing. She had long brown hair that twined and tangled in Caidin's beautiful silvery-white fur, and for a minute, Irene felt that she might be looking at herself, the ghost of her young self, the self who had not cut her hair, had not married Tom. The one who hadn't listened so closely to her mother, who would not let herself be eaten up by cancer and grief. Her hand went to her chest, feeling for the empty place. She felt invisible, caught in a piece of unfriendly time, unable to move toward Caidin or reclaim him.

But it was just a girl, of course, a girl who was studded with silver hoops, even her nose and her navel. Caidin, Irene called, and was sad to hear her voice so weak and quavery.

She heard a voice call back. Betty, it called, and she thought how strange it was to hear Caidin's voice after all this time, a gravely baritone, as if he'd been a smoker. He knew her old name, of course, there was no hiding anything from him.

The water was cold, like when her father filled the baby pool from the hose. Taylor had a hold of Laurette, and she splashed in the water. Swimming was like jumping or like lying down on the water while your legs kicked. See, she said to Laurette, but the water splashed up into her mouth. The water was foamy, like her bath water with bubbles in it, and it seemed like it was in a hurry to go someplace. Don't worry, Taylor said to Laurette, but she felt a little worried herself. She remembered baby Brooke who was supposed to be looking out for her. But maybe she had other stuff to do in heaven. Maybe she was sleeping. And anyway, what could she do? She was just a stupid baby.

■ ■ ■

Evie laughed. The dog was licking her, as if they had always known each other. She heard Roger call out, and ignored him. Aren't you beautiful, she said to the dog. Aren't you the prettiest puppy in the world.

Roger was calling out someone's name, not hers. Betty Ferris, he was calling. Is that you? Evie hoped Betty wasn't one of his wife's friends or she'd never hear the end of it. But who cares, she said to the dog, pulling his ears gently. The dog opened his mouth and took her hand gently between his teeth, pulling.

Roger and some old lady were talking, and she let herself be led away. Let him look for her, serve him right for paying attention to old Betty. She could have him, Evie thought, and as if she had been thinking of this all along, she knew she was going to break up with him.

With a great sense of relief, she followed the dog down the bank to the creek. On the grassy verge, a man was pulling off his shoes, calling out something. He struggled with the shoes, and when Evie came up to him, he turned to her and said, can you swim? My god, can you swim? I can't swim. He seemed prepared to jump in if she said no, so she told the truth. I was on the swim team, she said, and he pointed downstream. Something pink and white floating in the river, like a bouquet thrown away by a bride. It's Taylor, he said, my god, she's in the water.

Evie jumped in, and the dog followed her.

■ ■ ■

The far western portion of Hocking County drains into Raccoon Creek, which is in some places as deep as 30 feet, flowing eventually to the Ohio River. It's a geological phenomenon, one of several stream reversals caused by the glaciers. oldeforester.com

■ ■ ■

Betty Ferris? Not Caidin (of course!), but a man, heavy in the shoulders, brushcut hair. Is that you? he said. It used to be me, Irene said, and then added Yes, for clarity. It was someone she knew, or used to know.

Roger Hardesty, he was saying, and she found herself blushing, for she had known him in high school (how could she have forgotten?), Logan High School, all those many years ago. How nice, she said, remembering that he'd sat in front of her in her junior year history class, remembering even the plaid of his shirts drawn close over the muscle of his back, how his shoulders shifted when he slumped in his chair. It's Irene now, she said, but he didn't seem to hear her.

Betty Ferris, he said. What are you doing out here?

Walking my dog, she said. What about you?

Hiking, he said, but he seemed embarrassed.

Under his gaze, she felt first younger and then older, conscious of her thinned hair, her scrawniness. My dog, Caidin, she said, and looked around for him. He was gone, and so was the girl who'd been hugging him.

■ ■ ■

Evie cut through the water. She could see the child, a bundle of sodden clothes, ahead, bobbing up and going under. She came to the rapids and scrambled over the rocks, slipping on their algaed sides, the water foaming around her ankles. The dog dove into the deeper pool ahead, and she went in his wake, swimming as if she were lane-to-lane with her fiercest rival, Tiffany Lewis. She'd given it up when she hooked up with Roger—he often had free time when there was a practice. What was I, crazy? she thought. The water was like silk, or like Jello, and she moved through it with her powerful crawl (2nd place in State's).

She followed the curve of the river and when she came around the little bluff of trees the water smoothed out. She could feel the deep of it under her. The little girl and her pink and white clothes had disappeared. Evie looked to the white dog as if for advice. His eyes were blue, and they seemed to signal her. He bobbed his head and dove under the silty brown water.

■ ■ ■

Heaven was green, Taylor saw, green and ghostly, long trails of things coming up from the dark below. Brooke was waiting for her, and Taylor tried to shake her head. She didn't like the green, or the taste of the water in her mouth. She didn't like baby Brooke. Heaven was wet. Laurette's dress would be ruined. Dolls did not go to heaven, Aunt Amy said, and that was that. Dolls were not in the Bible, she said. But Laurette was here, so what did Aunt Amy know?

Taylor was tired, and her hair was drifting around her as she sank. The tangles would never come out.

■ ■ ■

In the Moonville Cemetery, I noticed that a lot of the graves we found were of the last name Jones.... A lot of the gravestones had "Asleep with Jesus" imprinted on them. The graves were surprisingly in very good condition for being well over 100 years old. home.fuse.net/Moonville

■ ■ ■

Irene brushed her hands down the front of her pants. How have you been? she said. She wished she'd combed her hair. I didn't recognize you at first, she said.

You've still got those green eyes, Roger said. Are you still married to what's his name? Tom?

Oh, no, Irene said. That's all over. She waved her hand. One of those things.

A man was running up from the river. He didn't have any shoes on, Irene noticed, which was strange. Have you got a signal? he said. Can you call 911?

She could see the child, a bundle of sodden clothes, ahead, bobbing up and going under.

I have a satellite phone, Roger said. What's wrong?

She's gone in the river, the man said. I just turned around for a minute and she was gone.

Who? Irene said, but they were already running down to the creek. Where? she said. The man gestured downstream, but there was nothing to be seen. Roger was talking into his phone, and the man started to run down the bank, pushing through the brush.

Irene's heart was beating fast. Where was Caidin? He wasn't in sight. Caidin, she called, but he didn't bark in answer. She'd lost so many things, she couldn't bear to lose anymore, not one more thing. Caidin, she called again, screaming as loud as she could. Roger, still talking on the phone, reached out and took her hand.

■■■

Evie followed the dog, but once under the surface she couldn't see much, just the silt hanging in the water like clouds in the sky, obscuring the light. The trees overhung the river, darkening the water. It felt as if night was coming, the dark night where the moon didn't reach. The moon in Moonville, which was silly, she thought. She came up for air, and the water spread around her as smooth as a plate, only the ripples of her surfacing to disturb it. She felt at home in the river, the water like thicker air, holding her up. She could hear voices from upstream, someone calling a word that sounded like "fading," as if they were commenting on the passing of the light. It would be night in a little while. She didn't find this displeasing, but she had to find the dog, and they had to do what they were there for.

■■■

There were at least four deaths near the tunnel, including a young girl who was killed by a passing train on the nearby trestle while going to visit a lover. ohiotrespassers.com

■■■

God was supposed to be in Heaven, Taylor thought, but he wasn't. No God, no Brooke. But there were angels, with teeth. One of them took her by the neck of her blouse and dragged her through the green cloudy light. She tried to say that it hurt but her mouth was full of water. She fell out of Heaven still holding Laurette and the angel pulled her along the surface of the sky. Someone put an arm around her and she and the angel pulled until she felt Heaven falling away, going down like the water in the tub. Her father stood ahead, holding out his arms, and Taylor was happy that he wanted to keep her with him.

■ ■ ■

When Irene and Roger got there, the brown-haired girl was bent over a child lying on the bank, water dribbling out of her mouth. The shoeless man knelt with his hands clasped as if he were in church. Caidin lay watching the girl press the water from the still, silent body and breathe into her mouth.

The paramedics are on their way, Roger said. They stood, hands hanging loose, unable to move, listening to the girl's ragged breathing, and the steady puffs of air she pushed into the little girl's mouth.

Oh, Irene thought, if anyone, it should be me. She ought to offer herself, she thought, to say, take me instead of this child. Roger was holding her hand, and she wanted to step away from him, but his hand was so warm, so almost familiar that she hesitated. It should be me, she thought, feeling the lightness and space next to her heart. But she couldn't pray for it, she couldn't give herself to the thought. She didn't want to give Death even this advantage, the edge of her selfless wish.

■ ■ ■

Taylor opened her eyes, although she hadn't realized they were closed. The sky was in the right place, the creek was beside her, talking to itself. Her father was crying, which men weren't supposed to do.

Do I know you? she asked the girl who had been kissing her. Her father was falling down on her, and she put her arms around him.

■■■

I'm Evie, she said to the little girl. Evie sat back on her heels, panting almost as hard as the dog. Her hair was probably a mess. She pushed it back from her face and looked around for Roger.

Are you OK? he said.

A lot you care, she said, but she couldn't help smiling. He was an asshole and it was over, but he wasn't so bad.

What's your name? she said to the little girl. She gave her the doll to hold, and its hard-lashed eyes clicked open. I'm Taylor, she said, and this is Laurette. She's been very bad, but it'll be OK after she goes in timeout.

Evie laughed. The white dog looked up at her, panting, his teeth gleaming. Water dripped from her hair. The creek kept sliding past them, coming down from Moonville. ■

ARCHEOLOGY

We excavate the evening
where a herd of staghorn sumac move slowly at the
    edge of this forest
Tree frogs are singing in silhouette branches
while bees settle down to sleep inside the green shades
of the poplar's fat flower

We excavate the evening
measure out each moment with Zeno's arrow
so the future can never invade the present
and the present can never escape
into the past

We excavate the evening
and like trees turn it over slowly in our hands
Depth we see is the great mistake
What we really seek walks here at the surface
like insects striding across the water at twilight

ERIK REECE

THE LAST MANIFESTO

A red-tail hawk clings in the wind
to a road sign twenty-nine miles from Knoxville

A bur oak stand in an empty pasture
like a character from some half-forgotten alphabet

a sign trying to call our attention
back to the thing itself

Then a flock of birds I thought were dead leaves
rise with one will

out of the tree's highest branches
and disappear against the horizon

The oak's empty limbs scatter twilight
across the field of snow

a sign that there will be no signs
just the birds vanishing in flight

and the dark branches writing on the wind
a bur oak manifesto

ERIK REECE

THINKING ABOUT RACHEL CARSON IN FLORIDA

The wave is an ancient architecture
always rising and dissolving
back into its own element

The sands on this beach were once Appalachian mountains
waves themselves slowly brought low
and delivered down to this delta

where the years crushed them into quartz
as if to prove that time is not an arrow called progress
and its target is not a destination called *at last*

ERIK REECE

DEAD LETTER TO LI PO

I think you would like
this narrow trail
that leads under

the tangled crowns
of rhododendron
then around Laurel Mountain

where galax blooms
among bracken fern
and float stones

Even if this range
is just an accident of uplift
the work of the earth's

crashing plates
still my mind feels at home here
among this shifting fog

and these green hills
that gather clouds and
turn them into rivers

I know it is my restlessness
that draws me
to these mountains

these elemental certainties
of scarlet oaks clinging
to grey boulders

I do not know what lies behind
this impulse to turn
the world into words

this walk
into lines on a page
Except that the words

are a way back
to the world
and on good days

I can forget
where the page ends
and the real poem begins

ERIK REECE

SILENT SONG

SUSAN TEKULVE

In Camerota, where the locals dance salsa every night for all of summer in a club called The Cyclops, I step into the butter yellow church in the piazza and find the most sorrowful Madonna I've ever seen. She stands on the right side of the altar, her eyes red-rimmed, her young face pale, haggard, shining with sweat. Wearing a brown gown adorned with a few rustic stars, she gazes wearily toward the heavens, a hotel hand towel draped over her right arm as if she's laundered linens all day beneath Mediterranean sun. Her bare feet are bound by single black straps of leather sandals, and the sacred heart pressing down on her chest looks as heavy as the steering wheel of an ancient boat. Her crown appears as if it's been tossed to the ground beside a patch of lilies. Plucked of their white blooms, the stems rise like ditch weeds from the rocky earth around her.

There are no other visitors in San Domenico, the mother church of this town on the Cilento coast of Southern Italy. A local charwoman beats the floor with fierce, muscular strokes of a stick broom. Haloed by clipped white hair, the sweeper's face is angular and serene, barely flushed from her labor. She bears little resemblance to the woman who must have modeled for the sorrowful Madonna. The model for the statue must have been used twice because her image was recycled into a second version of the Madonna placed on the left side of the alter. The second Madonna's brow has been dried of sweat, and she's adorned with lace and crown. A crowned infant Christ settles on her hip, a white ribbon tied around his wrist, a crucifix dangling from its end. This Madonna's feet are unbound from the black-strapped sandals, her toenails painted silver, but her brown eyes remain red-rimmed, weary. They look directly out, as if she knows already the weight of crown and crucifix.

The two statues of the Madonna must be effigies for all the mothers of Camerota who knew the weight of sons lost during La Miseria, a time of unimaginable poverty in early twentieth-century Italy, when seven million peasants and day laborers emigrated to North and South America, when 87% of those leaving were from Southern Italy. My own maternal grandfather, son of tenant farmers from Palermo who emigrated to the States during the depths of La Misera, when two-thirds of the island emigrated, never spoke about it directly. Whenever I asked about the country his parents left behind, he said, "C'era una volta," *once upon a time*, over and over. He said, "If you drop a heel of bread, you pick it up, and kiss it."

The mothers of Camerota kissed their sons before they sailed to Caracas to become thriving merchants, importing salami, olives, tinned tomatoes. Later, the mothers began fearing the bullets of political unrest in Venezuela more than famine. They feared the men would marry Venezuelan women and have children, leaving the women of Camerota to die in a paese fantasma, a ghost town filled with only the old and infirm. They called their sons home to marry Italian women. The men made several crossings in the 1940s and 50s, bringing back Spanish boats and dances, food, wives and children, South American street names and saints.

Mingled among the suffering Madonnas in the mother church are a painting of a shipwreck in a storm and statues of Saint Gerard Majella, Saint Domenico di Guzman, and Saint Louis Gonzaga. All South American men who left the safe harbors of their families to become great wandering monks in Italy, all three died of religious austerities, fatigue from excessive pilgrimages. The mother church keeps these religious figures with the collective memories of the town, its history of suffering and migrations. I've heard that this history is the reason the Italian-Venezuelans of Camerota are particularly friendly to foreigners, especially the African migrants, recent refugees from poverty and wars who've been crossing the stretch of Mediterranean between Libya and Southern Italy in what has become the world's greatest refugee crisis since the Second World War.

In April 2013, a boat carrying migrants from Eritrea, Somalia, and Ghana from Libya to Italy sank off the coast of Lampedusa, drowning over 360 people. The Italians responded by creating Marc Nostrum, which means "Our Sea," a military and humanitarian rescue operation that offered medical treatment, food, and legal aid for those seeking asylum. Though it saved an estimated 130,000 people, Mare Nostrum ended after a year, on October 31, 2014. The cash-strapped Italian government could not sustain its nine-million-euro-a-month budget. Factions of the European Union that opposed the rescue operation believed that the Italians were creating a "pull factor," encouraging more immigrants to make the dangerous sea crossing, thereby sentencing them to death at sea.

The mother church keeps these religious figures with the collective memories of the town, its history of suffering and migrations.

But isn't this "pull factor" only half the reason for most mass migrations? What about those who are pushed by desperate circumstances from their home countries? In November of 2014, Mare Nostrum was superseded by Operation Triton. Run by the European Border agency Frontex, Triton focuses on border patrol, and functions on a budget of three million euro a month, relying upon voluntary contributors from EU members and nonmembers, mostly smaller countries like Ireland, Portugal or Malta that feel in sympathy with the migrants and Italy.

Outside the mother church of the Italian-Venezuelan town of Camerota, June sun heats the cobblestones in the piazza. Morning swallows shriek, dodging dark pink bougainvillea that cloaks the arched door of a café across the piazza from the mother church. Coffee cups clank from within, and the bakery next door perfumes the air with powdered sugar. The locals dust sugar over everything they eat for breakfast: cream puffs, biscotti stuffed with almonds, hazelnuts, and citrons. They powder and slice cornetto, fill them with wildflower honey taken from bees that gather pollen from passion flowers growing on the Cape of Good Fortune, the rocky arm that embraces the marina where tipsy boats glide through swells of sapphire water into grottoes called "Love" and "Cathedral."

The children and grandchildren of the boatmen who crossed and re-crossed the Mediterranean have transformed themselves into merchants and artisans. On the Lungomare Trieste, the vendor's street above the marina, I step into a shop and find a case full of bracelets that look like small, silken fishing ropes. The merchant speaks in Italian peppered with Spanish, explaining how she was raised in Venezuela by a mother and grandmother who clubbed sea grasses with a baton into ropes used by sailors. Made to honor the work of the mother women in her family, the bracelets are soft, the color of dried oregano. They resemble the sea grass ropes that women in black kerchiefs stretch along cobblestones in the oil painting of old Camerota set artfully behind the bracelets.

The merchant walks me through her shop, opening each glass case filled with a lovely wonder she's fashioned with her hands: an amber necklace meant to resemble driftwood curving along a petrified piece of driftwood, earrings the color of sapphire draped over a framed postcard of the sapphire water flowing into the opening of a local grotto. She explains how each piece of jewelry chronicles an element of her family's history, which is really the village's history of migration—the push from starvation and joblessness toward work and food in Caracas, the eventual pull back to this safe harbor in Southern Italy, where the rocky cape slopes into a good-tempered sea that endlessly cradles and carves the stone into grottoes.

Walking through her store is a little like floating through the sea grottoes inside the nearby Cape of Palinuro, where sunlight siphons from chambers beneath the water, stoking it into an ethereal blue that looks like the beginning of creation. As you nudge your boat around each corner you must blink and imagine wondrous shapes—a dolphin's head or monks in prayer formed by stalagmites, a whole nativity scene sketched by water and age within walls streaked silver with sulfur. We turn another corner in the store, and reach a case filled with necklaces strung with Chiclets. Yellow, green, orange, white, and pink stones shaped like teeth, they remind the merchant of the gum she bought from markets in Caracas when she was a child. She strings them into "treasure necklaces," hiding mother-of-pearls, polished sea glass, tiny hummingbirds and orchids carved from Italian coral between the colorful stones.

The merchant is small, sturdy. She flits to the very back of the store. There she dips head and hands into a case filled with her most treasured pieces, sleek drops of obsidian suspended within whispery thin treble clef pendants, a bracelet of lava rock moons surrounded by haloes of silver. The black jewelry blends harmoniously with the black notes on a piece of sheet music she's placed in the back of the case. The music is called "Silenzio Cantatore," *Silent Song*, her favorite Neapolitan barcarole, a boatman's chant whose rhythms imitate the strokes of a paddle. I read a portion of the lyrics, a sad and romantic folksong about a wounded Italian soldier on a faraway battlefield, pining for his lost love: *Maria, in the silence, in the melodious silence, I don't tell you the words of love, but this sea tells you them for me!*

Beside us, the window holds the mid-morning light at a distance. I realize that I'm in the presence of an artist with a talent for weaving a longing for her family's South American history with gifts from the Italian earth and sea. I realize, too, that there's no way to honor this woman's work with a significant purchase, no way to repay her for all the stories she's given me. Already, I've spent too much of her time, and I feel that I should buy something. But I've spent most of my cash at the bakery near the mother church, on a cornetto and a bag of cookies stuffed with almonds, hazelnuts, and citrons. I need to save the rest for my taxi ride back to Pisciotta, the neighboring fishing village twelve miles north where I've been living for the last week.

I have enough change for a postcard. I select one that looks like an oil painting of a scene from old Camerota called "Lavorazione dell' erba," herb work. In it, a woman sits on a wooden bench beside the old taverna, holding a baton over a bundle of grasses. Surely this muscle work was heavy and unending. Signs of La Miseria surround her, yet she's much more beautiful than the haunted Madonnas inside the mother church. Her body softened and aged by motherhood, her abundant breasts hang loose inside her rustic blouse, and her legs are swathed in a pale blue skirt that's ripped down one side. The harsh sun has darkened her neck and arms into the deep brown of her baton. Her bare toes curl comfortably in the dirt beside the stone as she gazes at the grasses she's about to pound. Her face is burnished, as if lit from within by the belief in the usefulness of her work.

She studies me, then sifts through the shells, picking up one after another, discarding several more before she pulls out an alphabet cone shell mottled brown and white...

I buy the postcard. The merchant smiles, begins rooting around in a basket on the floor beside the cash register. She studies me, then sifts through the shells, picking up one after another, discarding several more before she pulls out an alphabet cone shell mottled brown and white, the slender opening along its side a deep coral pink.

"I want you to have something from here," she says. "For listening."

On the way back to Pisciotta, I talk to the taxi driver, Memmo, a native of Camerota. Tall and barrel-chested, his face looks as if it were chiseled from one of the local cliffs. He's transformed his own car into a taxi, and hung a tiny green gym shoe from his rearview mirror along with his cab license. For the price of a two-way cab fare, he's tossed in a personal tour of his hometown. The green shoe swings wildly as he drives the winding road between sea and cliffs, one hand on the steering wheel, the other pointing out all the beaches, bays and natural arches we speed past. "Guarda!" he says. *Behold!* As he relates, the beaches of Camerota are the cleanest in the region. The bays are the deepest. The natural arches are the highest. Above all, I must return that evening to dance the salsa all night long at the Cyclops Club because it will be the most fun I'll have my entire time in Italy.

I explain that I won't be returning to dance the salsa that night. This disappointing news silences him for a moment, so I show him the postcard of the herb worker with hopes of reviving the conversation. "My Babo did this, " he says, explaining that his mother was from Venezuela, that she clubbed grasses into fishing ropes in the harbor like the woman in the postcard.

Just outside Camerota, Memmo halts the cab, and picks up a young woman walking along the road. She's African, a recent migrant. She's walking away from Camerota, wearing the uniform of a domestic, heading toward a few holiday villas in the neighboring hills above and below Pisciotta. A guest worker, the girl lives safely away from the barely habitable reception centers farther south in Italy and Sicily. Still, she has at least ten more miles to walk before she reaches Pisciotta, and it's the Mezzogiorno, the hottest part of mid-day, when the locals lock up shops and cafés in order to drowse through the heat.

Memmo's offer is robust, but the girl argues gently with him in fluent Italian accented with French. Memmo wants to give her a free ride all the way into Pisciotta. She refuses with a laugh and a firm, "No, I can walk the rest of the way." As the Italian cab driver and the African girl argue amiably for another mile, I sense that Memmo feels bound by the same history of migration. I sense that the girl feels less of this affinity with Memmo, much less at home here. When we reach a fork in the road, the girl wins the argument, and Memmo releases her from the cab.

The road to the left is an easy coastline road that leads down to the Marina of Pisciotta; the road to the right climbs an incline toward the town's historic center that lies near the summit 650 feet above. The girl closes the taxi door, heading right, climbing the road up the cliff. I suspect that she'll clean houses all afternoon and evening, and maybe walk the road back to Camerota after dark.

We continue driving, Memmo casting fatherly glances through the rearview mirror until he no longer can see the girl. When she disappears entirely, Memmo shakes his head, his broad shoulders hunched in defeat and bewilderment.

"That was very kind," I say.

"Kindness is not expensive," he says. "What does it ever cost to be kind?" According to the International Organization for Migration, in the year since Mare Nostrum was replaced by the less-generously funded Triton Operation, deaths at sea between Africa and Southern Italy have risen nine times. In April 2015, an Italian naval ship attempted to rescue a boat packed with 800 migrants. Those on the upper deck leaned toward the Italian ship, and capsized their own boat. Twenty-eight survivors were pulled from a sea of bodies. The dead not found in the water were discovered locked in the boat's lower hold.

Thousands of migrants continue to arrive daily from such places as Algeria, Egypt, Somalia, Niger, Senegal, Mali, Zambia, and Ghana. Many have been forced onto death trap boats at gunpoint by smugglers working the ports of Libya. The concrete reception centers on Lampedusa and in Calabria bulge with migrants who await papers, jobs and housing in more affluent cities in Northern Europe. The harbors of Sicily and some towns on the Southern-most coast of Italy have become graveyards of splintered, unseaworthy boats.

Now that I've spent a day among the lively migrants of Camerota, the medieval village of Pisciotta looks as still and ethereal as a ghost town tucked into a swath of olive groves near the cliff's summit. Memmo and I drive the rest of the way in silence, and he drops me off in the empty piazza. In my room, I sit near its only window overlooking the terracotta rooftops of villas sleeping within the silvery- green olive trees lacing the cliff that slopes to the sea. I pull out the shell given to me by the merchant of Camerota. I've since read that the snails that live within this sort of shell use a venomous tooth to harpoon and paralyze their prey. It's best to handle the live ones with care. Now emptied and removed from the sea, it's a perfect cone, its slender opening the color of a healthy ear. I run my finger through it, wondering if the unspeakable dangers from the African girl's past have left her unable to accept the present kindness from the Italian taxi driver. Was it the "push" from her home country or the "pull" of Italy that brought her here? Wouldn't it be better to think of the Mediterranean again as "our sea," rather than a plank of lethal water between Libya and Italy that must be policed? How much would it cost if more, and more affluent, countries from around the world reached out a kind hand to assist this historically cash-poor region of a single, small country in the European Union?

I watch the lapis blue swells from the deep push toward the pale green shallows near the harbor, mingling, pulling the weaker water back into the sea. If the sea is telling me the answers to any of my questions, I'm too far above the shore to hear it. Instead I hear the Breath of Africa, a wind that blows through the villages of Southern Italy in summer, casting a spell of melodious silence once believed by ancient mariners to be the song of sirens. ■

CEMETERY

At eighty-one, she bends bottom to sky, a full
forward fold. The heavens fall around us, rain rolls

to the river. We adorn each grave—husband, son—
with a pine wreath, a red bow, and a dollar store flashlight

to glow on Christmas Eve. I watch, my mother prays,
and my grandmother fiddles with the old Easter flowers.

Prayers are useless without action. She knows
what must be done. Bow before the river, bow before

the dead. Maintain a strong and healthy back.
Bend like the river, accept what is.

Rain is just rain. Grief is the remainder
of blessing. Let it fill you like the rain

fills the river, a familiar hand on the low back,
cool water slipping up memory's fleshy shore.

JENNIFER NEWHOUSE

AUDRE LORDE WAS A SECRET HILLBILLY: A LITURGY FOR THE 21ST CENTURY

Lorde, who would have turned 82 last Thursday.
If she had not died in that year of the rising Clintons, 1992.
If she had not battled for 14 years before that
breast cancer
liver cancer
For 58 years before that
the cancer of a disappearing mother
the cancer of being closeted
the cancer of being afraid.
Lorde, who saw face-front mortality's *merciless light,* who saw well in that light her own shame, her own silences, who warned us
with every one of her last breaths that *our silence would not protect us:* Lorde, who tried to protect us by speaking words.
For you learn when the stench of death is upon your own body, or the bodies of those you know, that death waits for no tongue to lift.
For you *become strong by doing the things you need to be strong for.*

For *this is the way genuine learning takes place,* Lorde says.
For Lorde, feeling was knowledge. More than thought.
For when you uncover what you feel, you will no longer be satisfied with pain.
No longer satisfied with despair.
With exhaustion.
Abuse.
Or lying to yourself.
Lying.
Lorde, who taught: we have learned to work when we are tired, and so we can learn to speak when we are afraid.

Who acknowledged she was tired.
Who acknowledged she was afraid.
For the master's tools will not dismantle the master's house.
For the U.S. is now an oligarchy.
Controlled by a corporatocracy.
For it has been since 1992.
For hillbillies have been since before 1902.
For hillbillies know the future of corporate rule: contemporary ancestors, my ass.
For hillbilly is the name of those who know the pecking order of the camp, where the boss's house sits.

Look up!
For we have broke our necks looking up.
For we have shed blood together   together
black, white, red, blue, brown, woman, man
for we, for you
in another time not unlike this time
tied the red bandanna around your neck
red neck
and fired your million rounds into history
each bullet whispering to the inside of corporate heads:
no human will ever be owned   *again.*
For you climbed into the bulldozer's mouth
choked it
for you sat in the mud and rain and rain starving
for you stood your bleeding bruising thinning body up
and strapped the dynamite across the dollar mounds
for you lit the match.
For you this you who is your ancestor
For she for he   knew

the kind of work that is a *travesty of necessities,* Lorde says.
by which we earn bread or oblivion, Lorde says.
For you were born into this place, native now to this place, and so you inherited knowledge in the genes
of the zip-code you now need
to be *deliberate and afraid of nothing*
or what Lorde would say again: that it is not profitable to be deliberate. But life is short
and we must make our choices. We must make the choice.
It's *The Listeners.*
Tell them I came, and nobody answered. That I kept my word
de la Mare says and Lorde memorized, recited those words to herself when she was a child, an incantation.
Do you understand?
It's not about you.
Except that it is.
When a poem says *I* --- it says *I* and it says *you.*
It's the union
and the union calls us
for your silence will not protect you.
Lorde, who came to believe inside each of us is a place, *ancient and hidden.*
Lorde the *black, lesbian, mother, warrior* Harlem-ite who was afraid of the South (until it made her)

Lorde, who became finally herself in the South
Lorde, who told us *poetry is not a luxury* then lived
and died like it was true
Lorde, who warned us.
If our lives became defined by profit   we will pay high.
We will pay out with our only dowry, that unalienable power   our human-ness.
We will hand it right over.
We already have.
Lorde, who left us instructions   *steal it every bit back.*
Life is real short, she said. Feel something, she said. Say something.
she said.
she said.
she said.

REBECCA GAYLE HOWELL

AN *APPALACHIAN HERITAGE* INTERVIEW WITH

CRYSTAL WILKINSON

In the introduction to her debut short story collection *Blackberries, Blackberries,* celebrated fiction writer Crystal Wilkinson drew a strong connection between two parts of her identity. "Being country," she wrote, "is as much a part of me as my full lips, wide hips, dreadlocks and high cheekbones. There are many black country folks who have lived and are living in small towns, up hollers and across knobs. They are all over the South—scattered like milk-thistle seeds in the wind."

It's been sixteen years since those powerful words first appeared in print, and in that time Wilkinson has crafted an influential, genre-spanning body of work that further reinforces her observation. *Water Street,* her second collection, was a 2003 Long-List Finalist for the Orange Prize for Fiction—one of the United Kingdom's most prominent book awards—and a Short-List Finalist for The Hurston-Wright Legacy Award. Her work has been widely anthologized and published in respected literary magazines including the *Indiana Review, Slice,* and *Pluck!*. In March, her highly anticipated novel *The Birds of Opulence*—a lyrical exploration of how several generations of small-town black women deal with mental illness—was published by the University of Kentucky and excerpted in the *Oxford American.*

Wilkinson recently sat down with her longtime friend and colleague Silas House and discussed her new novel, craft techniques, talking country, and how owning an independent bookshop has influenced her literary life.

■ ■ ■

SILAS HOUSE: What do you want readers to know about *The Birds of Opulence*?

CRYSTAL WILKINSON: I see this book as a sort of a meditation. It's not written linearly. A lot of people would describe it as a story written in vignettes, and I did that intentionally to replicate memory. It's about the things that we carry forward. On the cover of the book Ron [Davis, Wilkinson's partner, who is a poet and visual artist] did this wonderful design of the Sankofa bird, which comes from

Africa. And it's about what we carry forward and what we pick up from our past, like remembering where you come from. So I think that the book is about those things, sometimes hurtful things, that are passed down from generation to generation—some of them things that we can do something about, like abuse in families, and some of it you can't do anything about, like what's inherited, like mental illness.

SH: That's one thing I definitely wanted to talk about—the theme of mental illness that runs throughout. Was that difficult for you to tackle, or was it cathartic to write about that?

CW: I think it's always been something difficult for me to write about. And I write about it from a personal standpoint because it's something that has been prevalent in my family, and something that is prevalent I think throughout Appalachia and up hollers and across knobs that people just don't talk about directly. And I think that's why I wrote it in the vignettes.

SH: One thing I loved about the book is the way you play with point of view. For example, the book opens with the narrator describing the day of her birth while still in the womb. And then throughout the book you use the omniscient voice, which is notoriously hard to pull off, and you do it just beautifully. I think it's one of the best things about the book. Can you talk a bit about that process, and why you chose those approaches?

CW: From a craft aspect it was hard to wrangle the omniscient point of view, and I couldn't really get a hold on it until I used my own metaphor and my own theme to kind of

Crystal Wilkinson

grapple it, which was the idea of a bird. And so I decided that in my narration that the omniscient point of view wouldn't go all the way up to the heavens—that it would only go up as far as a bird could fly over this community, and...I imagined that the bird would come down and light next to a character or sometimes sort of metaphorically be inside the character. And that's the tool that I used to try to control it...And then the idea of the character narrating from the womb came about in thinking about ancestral memory—and not just the memories that we have in the known world from the time of birth, but the idea that from a spiritual realm perhaps there are memories that are embedded inside us as a spirit even before we're born.

SH: [The] idea of collective memory?

CW: Yeah.

SH: It seems to me that there is also a lot about shame throughout the book. Would you say this is a profound issue for you as a writer because you come from two very distinct cultures—rural culture and black culture—both of which are cultures that are taught by larger society to be ashamed of being who you are, of...being seen as throwaway people or people who are inferior? Or am I just reaching here?

CW: No...I think you're right. I think that idea of shame is something that, again, [is] prevalent in Appalachian communities, either from the inside point of view, or particularly from the outside point of view—*you need to get that out of you, you don't need to talk that way, you don't want people to think this about you.* And I think that having children out of wedlock—there's a particular shame that comes with religion. There's a particular shame that comes from a small town mentality of being that girl in town that has a reputation or…putting shame on your family and those kind of things. And those were all issues that I wanted to write about collectively. So yeah, absolutely shame is a big part of the book. And I think it's a big part of community, so I sort of stuffed all of that together and tried to write about it.

SH: I've always been a big fan of your writing, as you know, but I think this new book takes your work to a whole new level. You really do seem to be at the height of your powers in the novel. It's so lyrical. Would you say that that lyricism is something that was just organic in writing this book, or [did] you spend a lot of time worrying over each sentence? Or [was it] a combination?

CW: I think it's a combination…Once I made the decision to fully be a fiction writer I fought against the poet in me all [the] time, and this is the first time where I allowed her to be fully herself...at one point this book, which is a very small novel, was much larger. And so I spent about a year condensing it back down, actually worrying over the language and distilling it, and distilling it, and distilling it down and revising it in the way that I would a poem, sometimes trying to read a line to see about the syllables before a comma, what should go there, how many words [could] I take out. I did a lot of work around word choice and around sentence structure, syntax, and diction.

SH: It sure does show—it just has such a wonderful flow about it that often it just feels like it's, it's just coming out of you, that lyricism and that natural poetry that you have

about yourself. But at the same time, I'm always trying to teach my students that, even if it comes out and it feels so like you've got it in that organic sense, you still have to go back in and worry over it. And I—the longer I'm a writer, the more I love revision. I used to fight against revising so much. Would you agree with that?

CW: Oh, absolutely. I mean I think that's the best part, you know I talk about that in my classes, too—you've made this thing, and there it is. And I think that's the hard part—it's like giving birth, and then you get to play with it and...make these either small decisions or grand decisions. I always say you have to either apply a bulldozer, or you have to know when you need brushstrokes, and getting in there line by line, sentence by sentence, and doing that is the fun work. That's the hard work, but I also get a lot of enjoyment out of it.

SH: Would you talk about the symbolism of the birds [that] show up in many ways throughout the novel? I know you said that it was in some ways a device that you used, but there's just so much bird symbolism. You mentioned that the book cover is a nod to...African [symbolism].

CW: It's an African Adinkra symbol that shows up actually in a written language in some African tribes, particularly the Akan tribe. And the bird actually has a seed in its mouth and it's looking over its shoulder...It goes along with the saying, *you have to know where you're coming from in order to know where you're going*...And I tried to mimic that larger theme in the book, and it was just amazing the way that I started out with a metaphorical bird, and then all of a sudden all of these literal birds showed up in the book, which I think was a big nod to Casey County and...to the way that I grew up, the way that the birds kept coming...I grew up in a household that definitely believed in granny knowledge, and what the symbols of birds were—like if a bird gets in the house then somebody's in danger, and a lot of those things. And so even my grandmother would call somebody a bird—she would say, "That Chrissy sure is a bird." So I became obsessed with it, and I think birds show up just about every way that they can in the book, as a metaphor and literal birds as well.

SH: I've heard you say in the past that you have felt that those who write about the black rural experience are often particularly ignored in New York literary circles. Can you expand on that?

CW: [It] was that way when my first books came out. There was—I literally still have those letters, those early rejection letters, that actually say, "When she's ready to write something more contemporary, let us know. We like her characters, we like her language, but we want something more contemporary." Which at the time I think was the beginning of urban fiction, and that's basically how a lot of African-American writers were being pigeonholed into that genre of writing—urbanized fiction. I think it has unloosened a little bit, particularly with smaller presses. I've seen a lot more books with small presses that give a nod to the African-American experience in rural areas. But I'm not so sure New York still is printing those [kinds] of books—the large presses I don't think are paying attention.

SH: One thing that you and I have always had in common is a history of being judged based on the way we talk. Can you talk a little bit about the way people have reacted to your accent throughout your life?

Wilkinson's latest book was published in March.

CW: I've written an essay about this in *Back Talk from Appalachia* [a 2000 anthology edited by Dwight Billings, Gurney Norman and Katherine Ledford] that gets discussed a lot...Ever since I was a little girl it's been an issue, and I've become a code-switcher at times. I love the magic in your voice and how you stick to it no matter what you are, but I find myself being a chameleon—like I always am willing to change it depending on who I'm talking to because it's always been an issue. And sometimes I get tired of talking about it. So it's much easier for me to curve everything out and say "Well hellooo!" than it is for me to say "Hi" [pronounces it "haa"] or "Night" [pronounces it "naht"] or whatever and then have people gather around like I'm a bird in a zoo or something.

But I also think that what comes with that is that it's even more hurtful than making fun. Making fun is one thing, but when that extends to how knowledgeable you are, or whether or not you're intelligent, that's when it becomes an issue for me, a huge issue for me. And over the years, particularly when I taught in [Kentucky] Governor's School for the Arts, I would have students come in who had been trained and I would think, "Well, this kid can't possibly be from Appalachia, speaking like this." And then after two or three days they would go [she sighs deeply], "Well, finally I can refine my tongue, it's okay." But they thought that since they were coming down to Lexington or going to Louisville that they were gong to get made fun of if they didn't speak the Queen's English...Kids are always made fun of for something, which is horrible, but there's always something that kids find to make fun of each other about. But when you become an adult—or even when you become a young adult—it becomes associated with your level of intelligence.

SH: And it's so acceptable—

CW: Yes!

SH: —to blatantly make fun of somebody about that. I do code switch to some degree when I'm speaking in particular places, but the thing is I'm just so bad at it nobody can tell any difference.

[Both laugh]

SH: I can't make my mouth move [that] way. Speaking of dialect, you handle that in a really masterful way in *The Birds of Opulence*—so masterful in fact that I don't think most readers would even notice that you're doing it... You are completely showing the dialect, but you do it in a very subtle way—mostly by syntax and by the use of an occasional colloquialism. We usually see dialect more done with phonetic spellings. Did you think a lot about that while you were writing, or is that something that comes [naturally] to you?

CW: I thought a lot about that. I don't have to think about it as much as I used to, but if you look at my early books, I wrote phonetically. I always tell my students if you want to learn from a writer, read their first books—read their books in order and you can see what they were trying to do, and then you gradually see them doing it a little bit better. And I have to even say that for myself. I think I've worked hard—this book is not perfect, but there's a...big difference between the way that I used dialect in *Blackberries, Blackberries* and the way that I used dialect [in *The Birds of Opulence*]. A lot of that I learned from...James Still, Ernest Gaines, Lee Smith, Gayl

Jones—they're writers that I love and went back to time and time again to say to myself, "Well I'm doing this, and what I'm trying to do is this. Let me see how they've done it. And then how would my characters do this, how can I better pull this off?" So it's been a study over the years.

SH: Are you revealing what you're working on right now, or are you one of those writers that don't talk about that?

CW: I probably am one of those writers that talk about it too much.

SH: Me too.

CW: But I'm still working on a memoir about my mother and this continuation of black women and mental illness, but no longer cloaked in fiction—telling the truth of the legacy of mental illness in my family. And I'm even talking about—this is new, I haven't really told anybody about this—but I'm talking about my own depression and anxiety in this book. For the longest I thought that it was just about my mother and her sort of severe mental illness, but it's become more of a trilogy of talking about my own bouts of mental illness, with depression and anxiety, and talking about my daughter—she knows about this so I'm not outing her in any way—and also talking about my mother and this legacy... It's also sort of a meditative book. My agent wanted a full-on traditional memoir, and I've come to accept that I don't write that way anymore—I'm not really a linear writer...I love the fragmentation in writing sort of a hybrid piece.

SH: Has owning a bookstore changed you as a writer or as a reader?

CW: I think it's changed me as a reader. Ron [who manages the bookshop] actually curates most of the books based on what's popular and then what's kind of eclectic. So it's nice to be...at the bookstore and pick up something that I wouldn't ordinarily read and be captivated by something new that I hadn't given a chance before.

SH: And you all are having so many events—you're bringing in a lot of great writers...in your bookstore, so you're certainly hearing even more readings and talking to writers even more, so that must have an impact too.

CW: Yeah, absolutely it does. The idea of community—you know, everybody talks about the writer writes by themselves and you know you have this sort of romantic vision of the writer in their corner with their computer or their typewriter or their pen and their journal. And that's true, but you've got to live, you've got to have a lived existence. And I think if you're not out living and you're just in isolation writing, then you're not writing the truth...And I'm still a very shy person, a very reserved person, so it's...not easy for me to be in a room full of people, but I think it's essential and I love it. ■

LOST AND FOUND ON HIGHWAY 25 SOUTH

You've already forgotten why you've come. Why you left the mountains to be swallowed whole by kudzu, to become a wanderer in a desert of hand-scrawled signs, each one a temptation or a prayer: *Watermellons. Stop. Tomatos. Here.* There is no one place, only places scattered along the falling highway, as if each produce stand and clapboard church meant to climb the mountain but never made it. Farther down awaits the promise of respite, Travelers Rest having been raised up for people to stop in the evenness before the never-ending climb. But here, between the rest and the mountaintop, springs up an abundance of gaudy and God: every neon tinderbox selling fireworks followed by a church offering a backlit sign: *Are you ready?* Who wheeled these block letters and yellowed screens to the edge, only to then disappear along this now straight and empty and ever-growing stretch of nowhere? *Look up,* the next church demands. But you can't. You're still contemplating the majesty of the purple spires and striped green castle of Charlie's Fireworks. *Jesus,* the sign assures, *is coming*. And now you know. Not far beyond the pasture of ceramic animals, each one stilled as if life solidified in its blood, you realize: He has come already. No one is here; everyone has been raptured away into clouds and everything remade, the world a deep, hungry green, and soon, you are sure, The Dixie Outpost and Foothills Baptist Church and even Charlie's Fireworks will be wound tight in weeds and vines, leaving only words peeking out as if flashes of flesh beneath a tattered shirt. You will fall only farther down because there is no way up from here, no exit, no turnoff, and those coming behind you will find only traces of what was: *Look. Stop. Jesus. Fire.*

JEREMY B. JONES

FLOOD STAGE

TIM POLAND

The river had been low and sluggish for over a month at that point. The fishing had been good enough, but beyond that there hadn't been much at all for us to give a hoot about for some time. We felt about as sluggish as the river, mutely longing for something to get us churned up, thought you'd have a hard time finding anyone to admit that now. At the hydroelectric dam they didn't have but one turbine gate open halfway. The river depth was less than three feet, and the level of Denby Lake behind the dam was going down, too. Most anyone who knew anything about the water running through town knew this, or some version of it. Not one of us knew that Tommy Lyles was parked out behind the McDonald's, waiting for Jenna Sutphin to get off work. More than likely, Jenna Sutphin didn't know he was out there either.

Not until a lot later, once they found Tommy and he started talking, would anyone other than him and Jenna have even a little bit of an idea what went on out there that night. It's taken a while, but we've been piecing together a story, and there's a fair chance we got some of it right. Near enough to right to satisfy most of us.

The one and only lead police ever had came from Jenna Sutphin's co-workers, the last to see her. No one else could have known a thing. That it would be Tommy Lyles the cops should be hunting for didn't come as much of a surprise to the other girls who worked the counter with Jenna. He'd been coming in a lot lately. Always the same—quarter-pounder with cheese and a large Mountain Dew—then he'd sit in a booth near the counter and watch Jenna. Once he told her he thought she was pretty. She smiled, said "thanks," then shared a covert smirk with Lydie Walters when she turned away to the pass-through shelves to get his quarter-pounder. Only once, as far as anyone could tell, Tommy actually asked her out. She declined politely, with a smile, said she had other plans, maybe some other time. When she told Lydie about the invitation, later, on break out back, Jenna rolled her eyes and said, "as if." Lydie said, "total creep. And he's, like, old—must be, like, over twenty."

Once they caught him, all Tommy seemed able to say was that he loved her and to keep asking why that hadn't been enough. He never gave out too many details about what actually happened out back when Jenna got off that night, but it wasn't too hard to figure out. All told, Lydie was right. Creep. With a father like Buddy Lyles, how could he not be? But also just a pitiful fool, thinking love was a simple thing, painted in only one color. If he could just get her alone for a few minutes he could show her his love was real, sincere. And if his love was sincere, how could she possibly deny him? That should be enough. All any girl ever wanted or needed. It had to be.

When it wasn't, he shoved her in his car and drove off, looking for a place out of the way to further convince her. Along the river, we found out later. Most anything of interest or importance around here, sooner or later, works its way down to the river.

■ ■ ■

The river remained low and slow that night, a black mirror, shimmering through the trees along Landing Road, but that would change soon enough. The front moving up from the Gulf was going to make its entrance into the region by dumping a load of rain on the mountains upstream in North Carolina and then work its way up the spine of the mountains to us right here in the Hatcher River Valley. Before Tommy got to that spot along the river he had in mind, while Jenna was still either screaming, calling him a creep, or cowering against the passenger side door, terrified—even before then the engineers at the hydroelectric dam were getting ready to open another turbine gate, to increase the dam's flow, no matter how much it dragged down the water level of Denby Lake. In this way, they could run more of the coming flood through the turbines, generating more electric power, more cash, and waste less of that lucrative water through the flood gates above the spillway of the dam.

Jenna might have been screaming, might have been dumb with fear. We like to think she fought back. Truth is, we don't know. What Danny Pinsker and Stanley Sowers found wedged into that big sycamore snag just downstream from the intake valve at the water processing plant, well, it didn't look much like the Jenna Sutphin we knew. Thanks to fish and other critters, and to the flood, there wasn't all that much you could tell for sure from what was left. Only that she was strangled, the way her windpipe was crushed, and that she didn't drown. No water in her lungs, so she was dead before she ended up in the water. No chance of telling if she'd been raped or not. That little creep Tommy Lyles, by the time they pulled him out of that old camper trailer where he'd been hiding, he couldn't do more than babble on about how he loved her and that she should have loved him. That, and he'd left her body on the big island just this side of the interstate.

Of course, none of us knew this until Jenna had been missing for nearly two weeks, but it seemed to fit. Tommy would have taken her somewhere out of the way, along the river. Whether she screamed or cried or fought or sat in paralyzed terror, he would have thought she'd come around, give herself over to him, once she saw how much he loved her. When she didn't, he mashed his thumbs into her throat and cut off her air until she stopped screaming or crying or fighting or being terrified. Not able to think of anything else, he would have driven to that little turnout at the end of Fenton Street. No one down there to see anything that time of night. He'd have dragged her down the bank to the water, his footsteps slipping on that steep little footpath. By that time, the river would have likely been a good foot deeper, the current stronger from the increased water release at the dam. It would have been a strain for him to wade across the fork to the big island. He might have heaved Jenna's body over his shoulder or might just as well have let her float and tugged her through the water to the island. We won't ever know, and it's not like it matters now. One way or the other, he strangled that poor child, toted her body out to that island, and dumped it there, probably somewhere back in that stand of blackberry brambles where it would be harder to see. That much we can be pretty certain of.

Killing what you love because it doesn't love you back doesn't make any sense, at least not to most of us.

■ ■ ■

By the time the search got up and going, the rain had been on us for a couple days. At the hydroelectric dam they were running two turbine gates open all the way. That makes for a strong current, but nothing out of the ordinary. By all the forecasts, though, a load more rain was on the way. And it was. The river was just going to get deeper and stronger for some time, and we knew it. And it did.

Searching for something that isn't trying to be found, isn't hoping to be found, is harder than you'd think. Anyone who's lost a cat or a dog knows that. The first couple days, the police put most of their efforts into finding Tommy Lyles since that was all they had to go on. Jenna Sutphin was missing, they knew that for certain, and that Tommy was the last one to be seen with her. Lydie Walters made sure the police knew that. She'd seen that creep Tommy out in the parking lot when Jenna opened the back door to leave at the end of her shift. Lydie said she didn't see anything else because she had to get back to her station at the drive-thru window. Last we heard, Lydie hasn't been back to work since. Blames herself. Can't stop crying. Poor thing.

The police put the word out in all the official channels and looked for Tommy Lyles. They found his car parked in that alley out behind his parents' house, but his folks said they hadn't seen him in a couple of days. No surprise in that.

As for the other part of the search, we took care of that. A.J. at Peery Office Supply ran off all the fliers free of charge. Those fliers, with a recent photograph of Jenna on them, got plastered all over town—store windows, utility poles, a quarter-page ad in the *Dalton's Ferry Register*—but we knew they wouldn't make a lick of difference. We all knew who we were looking for. Still, it made us feel like we were doing something. When she was hobbling out of Meade's Supermarket, Edith Quesenberry saw one of those little Corbin brats draw something filthy on one of the fliers. Old and slow as she is, with that bad leg and all, Edith beat that Corbin kid senseless with a bag of cantaloupes she pulled out of her shopping cart. Marty Griffith said it was actually kind of funny—the Corbin kid lying there, stupefied, melon pulp all over the place.

Searching for something that isn't trying to be found, isn't hoping to be found, is harder than you'd think.

A little shrine for Jenna grew up outside the high school—cards, flowers, candles, stuffed animals—the usual stuff. A smaller shrine showed up behind the McDonald's, where she was last seen, but the manager had it removed. The delivery trucks couldn't get to the back door. That manager, he's not from here originally.

Prayers for Jenna were flying pretty thick in all the churches in town, especially at Zion Baptist, where Jenna's mother, Maureen, was a parishioner. How that woman has borne the weight, none of us can imagine—that rotten ex-husband of hers long out of the picture, the cancer she's still fighting, and then this.

Some of us went out looking, driving around town, up and down alleys, wandering along the river, but the rain made that part of it difficult. And folks couldn't stop going to work, going on with their own lives, no matter how awful it all was. You do what you can, which isn't much, but you do it anyway.

■ ■ ■

In the end, it was the flood brought things to a head. The hand of God, some of us said. Others said it was more like weather and the hands of the engineers up at the dam opening the floodgates. Closure, a few of us called it. Others of us thought things were still about as muddied up as they usually are after a flood.

We were well into the second week of steady rain here, and it had been even heavier upstream in North Carolina. The dam was already running all three turbine gates full bore, with more water guaranteed on the way once all that North Carolina run-off made its way downstream. Word was they'd have to open the floodgates any day now, and then there'd be one hell of a mess. And there was.

By the end of the second week of rain, the fliers about Jenna's disappearance were already looking tattered and worn and, as promised, the floodgates at the dam had to be opened. The river crested a good two feet above the fourteen-foot flood stage. Water got all the way up to the loading dock behind Meade's Supermarket. The foundry had to shut down, with a couple inches of water on the main shop floor and the parking lot completely underwater.

And the flood found Tommy Lyles.

The folks who live in the little houses and trailers along that part of Dudley Street that bends right down to the river had to evacuate, and you can be sure they hightailed it in plenty of time ahead of the flood. They'd been through that before. But it had been seven years since a flood this bad. Since then, Millie Fontenot had taken a pretty serious turn for the worse. Her husband, Francis, had been gone five years at that point, and all she had was her daughter, Cindy, to care for her. Bed-ridden as Millie was, Cindy called the fire and rescue squad to help her move her mother out of harm's way, though by Cindy's account, her mother was so close to the end at that point, she may as well have just left her to the flood. Cindy's always been kind of rough around the edges.

When fire and rescue got to the Fontenot house, floodwater was halfway up the backyard and rising. It was already lapping at the door of the rusted old camper trailer propped up on cinder blocks in the weeds out behind the house. The paramedics kept a wary eye on the rising water, as any of us would, while they lifted old Millie into the ambulance, and that's when they saw him. Tommy Lyles, hiding out in that broken down old trailer. He'd opened the door into the muddied up flood surging around the trailer and stuck his head out, a look of flat confusion on his face, wondering where in the world he was going to hide out now. Just as dumb as he was deadly.

The paramedics got Millie tucked into the ambulance, called it in, and pulled out onto Dudley Street to wait for the police to get there. Millie and the ambulance would be safe out there in the street for a good while yet. They wanted to wait for the police and see them get that squirrely son of a bitch. After the last two weeks in Dalton's Ferry, any of us would have wanted to see that.

■ ■ ■

After hammering us for all that time, the rain just stopped, not another drop for weeks after that. The hydroelectric dam had closed the floodgates, and the river was settling back into something like its normal course. The water level was still high and rough, but no longer a danger, as long as you weren't fool enough to go out on the river just yet.

Word is, Tommy Lyles confessed right away. As if. Still, it took a couple days of his babble about how love should be before they got anything specific out of him. We can't confirm it, but they say one of the cops, Linda Rifkin, waled on him pretty hard. Linda is a close friend of Maureen Sutphin, had been since grade school, plus she had two daughters of her own. None of us could really blame her, considering.

Seems he'd been holed up in that old trailer the entire two weeks. Wilbert Croke said the place reeked of mold and piss and that it looked as if he'd been surviving entirely on Mountain Dew and Pop Tarts. How he got that junk in there, no one ever found out. Or whoever sold it all to him wasn't

Didn't surprise anyone in Dalton's Ferry that power and money were still worth more than the body of a young girl.

about to admit it. Either way, eventually they were able to decipher enough of his babble to figure out he'd dumped Jenna's body on the big island.

Water was still too high, the current too strong to get out on the island. Most of it was still underwater. Local authorities tried to get the engineers at the dam to decrease the discharge, but there was still too much water in the river upstream from the lake. If they cut back any more than they already had, that water would pile up and they'd have to open the floodgates again. Didn't surprise anyone in Dalton's Ferry that power and money were still worth more than the body of a young girl. They said we'd have to wait another day or two before the water levels could reasonably be expected to come down.

Natural disasters aren't always so natural.

■ ■ ■

Technically, anything out in the river channel is the jurisdiction of the Department of Game and Fisheries, but there wasn't anyone of a mind to make a fuss over jurisdiction. When the flow from the dam finally dropped low enough—police, fire and rescue, fisheries—they all tugged on their waders and trudged through chest-high water out to that island, none of them too eager to find what they were looking for. It took most all day, but they covered every inch of that big island and found exactly what anyone who knew anything about flooding on the Hatcher River could have told them they'd find after a flood like this one.

Nothing.

Jenna Sulphin had been washed downstream. Most of us could have told them she would have been, but they had to start there. Had to start somewhere.

They did find a black visor with the McDonald's logo stitched into it hanging from a branch about ten or twelve feet up a tree at the downstream tip of the island. A bit of a miracle they found that, some folks said. So, they knew that much of Tommy Lyles's babble was true. He'd taken her to the island, and she'd still been wearing her work clothes. As far as most of us could know, she could have been washed downstream most anywhere in such a flood. Game and fisheries would bring in their boats, and they'd start the search downstream first thing in the morning. That's as much as any of us knew at that point.

■ ■ ■

The next morning, at first light, game and fisheries had their boats, four of them, at the put-in ramp at the far west end of town, just downstream from the dam, just upstream from the big island. The police were there, fire and rescue, too. All of us knew this, and some of us made it down to the boat ramp to see them off, to wish them good luck, considering the circumstances. A few others of us were wandering along the riverbank, snooping half-heartedly for what we really didn't want to find, not having much else to do with ourselves but wanting to be able to say we'd helped with the search. Most of us, we were off to work or school like any other day.

The river was down, but still running deep and fast. More significantly, for the first time in nearly two weeks, the water had cleared, all that silt and mud finally settled out. Clear enough now to see a good ways into the depths. Clear enough to fish again. More than clear enough for Danny Pinsker and Stanley Sowers to justify slacking off on work that morning in order to get a line in the water—not something that would come as a surprise to anyone who had lived in Dalton's Ferry for longer than five years. On any given day, if the conditions were right, we could as likely as not expect to find Danny and Stanley out on the river, bass fishing. And anyone of us who knew anything about the river and the fish in it, which is most of us, knew that Danny Pinsker was the best damned fisherman on the Hatcher River. River guides from around the region have been known to follow him and Stanley, watching them through binoculars, trying to learn Danny's special spots. Stanley used to say that Danny Pinsker had the personal home address of every smallmouth bass in the Hatcher River Valley.

We understood that the search team had to do it by the numbers, start at the tip of the big island and work their way downstream, slowly, carefully, covering every bit of the river.

This was serious, and they couldn't cut any corners. We also knew that if they'd asked Danny Pinsker he could have told them that with flood water like that, the current would have swept over the big island and washed anything not rooted there in a wide arc out toward the main stem. The main current would have driven the secondary current back toward the bank until it cut around the shoal behind the foundry. After that, once it hit the rapids near those big boulders, it was anyone's guess which way something in the water would be carried off, but either way, it wasn't likely what they were looking for would turn up anywhere upstream from the water processing plant. If they'd asked, Danny Pinsker could have told them that.

Afterwards, Stanley said that he couldn't be sure, but it seemed like Danny knew they were going to find what was left of Jenna Sutphin that morning, that it was as if he headed right for the spot. They'd put in at the ramp by the park, and Danny had pointed his jon-boat right downstream. Stanley had to admit, they often started fishing by the water processing plant. A couple of good holes and grass beds there, usually thick with bass. And like they usually did, they'd started fishing there, and they'd each caught a couple right away. Good sized fish, all of them, scrappy and stirred up after the flood.

This is what made him wonder, Stanley had said. Normally, Danny Pinsker would never pull up and leave a spot where the fishing was that good. Never. Stanley said it was like he wanted to do something clean and good, no matter how briefly, before they had to face something that horrible. That it was like he knew. After landing those two good fish, bringing them in, holding them in his hand for a second before releasing them back into the water, Danny reeled in, laid his rod in the boat, pressed his foot to the pedal of the trolling motor, and guided the jon-boat slowly around that little bend until they saw that big sycamore snag and what was caught up in it. The search team would have still been a quarter mile upstream from the island at that point.

What Danny and Stanley found tangled in the half-submerged sycamore branches was so puffed and twisted it hardly looked human anymore. Stanley said he could hardly look at it, that he thought he was going to puke, it was so terrible. He said Danny never took his eyes off it.

Snarled up in that snag as the body was, the current was still strong enough that it might pull it loose and send it further downstream. Danny beached the jon-boat and got out to stay with the body while Stanley turned the boat upstream and ran it full throttle back to the boat ramp to try to flag someone down, have them call the police and tell them to get that search team downstream fast.

When Stanley Sowers drank too much, which was pretty often, he also talked too much, let out things that most of us would just as soon not have heard in the first place. As often as Stanley got drunk and chatty, he only told this last thing one time, as far as any of us can recall. But Brian McCraw was there when he told it, so of course, it got around. Stanley said that when he got back downstream to that snag, Danny Pinsker had scooted out onto the main trunk of that downed sycamore and was sitting right there on it, just above the body. He'd reached down into the water and taken hold of the swollen, purple lump of pulp that had been Jenna Sutphin's hand. And Stanley said Danny was just sitting there, leaned over sort of, holding that hand, not like he was holding the body in place but more like he was holding the girl's hand to let her know that she wasn't alone anymore, that nothing bad would happen to her ever again.

Brian said Stanley's hands started shaking then, that his eyes got all red and wet. He turned to Brian and asked,

"How in hell am I ever supposed to stop drinking after seeing something like that?"

For that question, not one of us had a good answer. ■

EPITHALAMION

On the blacktop road leaving

footprints in the roux of pollen they glance

at the black clouds ahead they glance

at each other and whelmed trees as if singing sway

he designs a proof for beauty it is her

nimbus of hair rising in the damp air now

broken piano keys appear in the sky

now some hand plays the diluvian music

now they know to begin running their throats

fill with water he is afraid of dying

yet there at the treeline an abandoned yellow bus

dividing the rain she pulls him there

and under the timpani under the speechless roar

her mouth finds his and under the iron-black branches

they say only the vowels and the shape of them

is left in the mud after the storm has passed

M.E. MACFARLAND

THE SMOKY SILENCE
OF MARY KARR AND CINDY SHERMAN

STEPHANIE BARTON

When a character in a narrative behaves erratically, her actions create a gulf of absence, even if she appears for breakfast every morning. A subject in a painting who looks away from the viewer amplifies the distance, whether she stands right in front of you or you watch her from afar. The void in these situations sets up a rewarding tension. Absence is a form of mystery, and in spite of ourselves—in spite of the danger—we want to peer into the abyss and find out what lurks there.

By carefully choosing scenes and dialogue, writers give dimension to characters and give readers a vivid sense of encountering definite, real people. In this way Mary Karr renders a portrait of her mother in her memoir *The Liar's Club* that is vibrant and specific. But because her mother has a habit of disappearing physically and emotionally—withdrawing into herself, choosing not to speak, and succumbing to drink as an escape—the reader is left feeling the character is only partially present. The mother is as impenetrable to the reader as she was to the narrator.

The women in the black-and-white photographs of Cindy Sherman's *Untitled Film Stills* inhabit a space where Sherman has intentionally placed distance between the subject and the viewer. Often the subject averts her gaze or angles her body away from the camera, or she stands slightly off center. The composition makes the photographs feel a little unbalanced, making the women elusive or just out of reach.

If we could measure absence by proportion in the visual and literary worlds (and in the real world) we might come up with a neat equation: the amount of space a character physically occupies versus the emotional space the character allows. Equal amounts of space would give a balanced character, but if she takes up too much emotional and physical real estate—she talks too much, she's around too often—we'd have a needy nuisance. A major character occupying too little space, though, would leave us feeling hollow.

■ ■ ■

A brunette pauses in the middle of a black room, holding a match to her cigarette. Light illuminates her cheek, a bright curve that glows in the deep gloom and seems soft beside the hard geometry of the cigarette. Her mouth turns down slightly as she peers at the match flame, her eyes masked in shadow. This is Cindy Sherman's *#32,* a black and white photograph of a woman frozen in a dark moment.[1]

Smoke and silence motifs are scattered across several of Sherman's *Untitled* photographs and through critical scenes of Karr's memoir. For both, a cigarette with a serene face embodies the idea of detachment, and smoke rising between people forms a diaphanous—but real—physical barrier. Sherman's photographs convey silence in the firm line of the mouth, by eyes cast away from the viewer. Both women also play on the ways focus and blur change the atmosphere in a scene.

Thus from the beginning Karr warns that her memory is uneven, reminding us along the way that her recollection of events can be fuzzy.

Karr structures her memoir, *The Liar's Club,* around snapshots from her memory she hopes to unravel. Her opening image is a moment in sharp focus contained within a dark envelope of memory, an isolated snapshot amid hazy details: "My sharpest memory is of a single instant surrounded by dark."[2] Much like the women in the Sherman photographs, Karr is caught in a moment, and time moves slowly around her.

Thus from the beginning Karr warns that her memory is uneven, reminding us along the way that her recollection of events can be fuzzy. But it's not just Karr herself who feels blurred: her portrait of her mother is that of a woman out of focus or trying to remove herself from the picture. Karr uses language that suggests omission to erode the mother-daughter bond: "The missing story really starts before I was born, when my mother and father met and, for reasons, I still don't get, quickly married."[3]

Smoke in Karr's memoir serves as a symbol for the haziness of memory, and actual cigarettes and smoke play as substantive a role in Karr's narrative as they do in Sherman's #32. Karr connects her mother with the smells of smoke and cologne: "I turned ... and entered the invisible cloud of odors that floated around mother at that time: Shalimar and tobacco and peppermint Life Savers."[4] The olfactory organs link to the limbic system in the midbrain, which is also the biological system associated with memory. Though smoke connects Karr to her mother in memory, it still constructs a screen that separates them:

> *A few times she would sit on the side of the bed all night smoking.... She had a way of waving away the smoke from my face and making a pleasant little wind in the process. I kept my eyes closed, knowing that if I roused she'd leave.*[5]

Karr breathes in her mother to form a bond with her, but she cannot touch her, and her mother is as changeable as smoke.

While Karr tells us that pieces of her story are missing, in particular, she is missing information about her mother. In describing her mother, Karr often turns to a strategy of presenting a sharp image that then blurs; throughout the book

1 Sherman, Cindy. *Untitled Film Still #32.* 1979. Museum of Modern Art, New York City.
2 Karr, Mary. *The Liar's Club: A Memoir.* (New York: Viking, 1995), 1.
3 Ibid., 10.
4 Ibid., 50.
5 Ibid., 56.

she sharpens—focuses on a remembered detail—then blurs scenes to create a sense of time swirling away.

Although Karr can supply details about her mother's life that give a sense of her personality—especially a brutal analysis of the mother's relationship with the grandmother: "She'd started auctioning Mother off to various husbands when she was only fifteen. Like some prized cow, Mother liked to say..."—these details still don't give the narrator the bond she hungers for.[6] The details fill out the character but they don't make a trusted relationship.

At the start of chapter two, Karr illustrates the narrator's gap in knowledge through the nondescript land of her mother's home: "If Daddy's past was more intricate to me than my own present, Mother's was as blank as the West Texas desert she came from."[7] Karr's sweeping assessment may overstate how little she knows (after all in the first chapter her father tells her parents' origin story and she outlines the lopsided relationship between the mother and grandmother) but her description provides a fitting visual that lays out the harsh emotional landscape she travels with her mother.

Sherman gives few clues about the women in her photographs as well, and that frugality heightens the mystery of her subjects. She's especially reticent about giving background details or landscape, and *#32* may be one of the starkest examples of her constraint. Sherman stands before an inky black backdrop where only the barest strokes of texture appear in the lower-left corner, a swathe of drapery flowing behind her. But the darkness of the backdrop—an abyss that would consume the subject if not for the match flame and the spot light—suggests a stormy mood.[8]

Karr expands on the parallel between her mother and the landscape of her mother's birth with the metaphor of a storm darkening over her family as they drive into a tornado: "Out in West Texas, the sky is bigger than other places. There are no hills or trees.... The scenery is blank, and the sky total.... So the sky getting dark was a major event, as if somebody had dropped a giant tarp over all that impossible brightness."[9]

Using the bland Texas landscape and the storms that sweep across it, Karr suggests that her mother perceives each stage of life as a blank slate. Her mother fills the slate with stories and then must wipe it clean before she can start the next stage; she must drive through all manner of psychic storms to put the past behind her and reinvent her life. Karr describes watching over her mother as a child and being aware that she could be wiped clean from her life, and her mother would not look back. Her suspicion is confirmed when she learns from her grandmother about half-siblings from a prior marriage:

> *And if they could be lost—two whole children, born of Mother's body just like us—so might we be. To believe that she'd lost those kids was to believe that on any day our mother could vanish from our lives, back into the void she came from, that we could become another secret she kept.*[10]

Karr presents the storm that could take her mother away in the form of her dying grandmother, who moves in and disrupts the unorthodox life of the family. Karr's mother withdraws when she finds herself under the grandmother's thumb again, and the elder's illness and eventual death dictate the mother's behavior. Karr lays her blurry film of detachment over that time, wrapped around sharp cold and silence: "Still, no matter

6 Ibid., 12.
7 Ibid., 23.
8 Sherman, *Untitled Film Still #32.*
9 Karr, 26.
10 Ibid., 80.

how bland a gaze you try to put on remembering an ugly illness... you will eventually stumble into a deep silence. And from that silence in your skull there will develop... a snapshot of cold horror."[11]

The silence troubles the narrator: it becomes her mother's identity. Karr cannot endure it: "I couldn't sit in her silence anymore. It just weighed too much."[12] Like the brunette in Sherman's *#32* studying the flame at her fingertips, the mother averts her gaze from her surroundings and focuses on the light directly in front of her. She avoids her family and excludes them from her experience. "Looking back from this distance, I can also see Mother trapped in some way, stranded in her own silence."[13] As Sherman's subject clamps her mouth shut around her cigarette, rejecting speech, Karr's mother refuses to communicate, choosing to internalize everything that is happening to her.

Karr wrote *The Liar's Club* while working as a poetry professor at Syracuse University; so she had put some physical and psychological distance between her childhood in Texas and her adult life. In an interview with Amanda Fortini for *The*

Through smoke-filled silence and blurred vision Sherman and Karr create women who have detached from their surroundings...

Paris Review, Karr speaks of her mother with some admiration, painting her as a more daring figure than the mysterious subject narrated by her childhood self: "I'd warned my mother and sister in advance that I wanted to cover the period of Mother's psychotic break and her divorce from Daddy... She was an outlaw, and really didn't give a rat's ass what the neighbors thought. She drank hard and packed a pistol. When I tested the waters about doing a memoir of the period, she told me, Hell, go for it."

Karr confirms, however, that her mother's wildness translated into a form of negligent parenting: "She wasn't that invested in child rearing. I was like a terrarium lizard you checked out from time to time with distracted curiosity."[14]

Through smoke-filled silence and blurred vision Sherman and Karr create women who have detached from their surroundings, from anyone who lingers near them, and from us as viewers and readers. By feeding us only scraps of details, both the writer and the artist succeed at isolating their characters. The elements of smoke and silence create a membrane around and between characters in their work. ■

11 Ibid., 49.

12 Ibid., 54.

13 Ibid., 55.

14 Karr, Mary. "Mary Karr, The Art of Memoir No. 1." Interview by Amanda Fortini. *The Paris Review*, Winter 2009.

WHO GETS KISSED

Is a new organic, open-pollinated sweet corn variety.
Also a game played at husking bees—shuck and shuck
the green papyrus off the pale yellow facets, search out
the red kernels to earn a kiss. The rules do not say
how many players, they do not say if the winner chooses
a partner or must endure the kisses of all participants.

I never played the game in all my time in rural PA
or anywhere in Indiana. I imagine I'd have to travel
farther west, the pretty snare of flatness, miles of milled
pavement and plant test plots and rare dog breeders.
She lurks in the half shadow of afternoon, the one
I never kissed, clean mouthed and young again,

before I moved away and she got pregnant
and married. Before she stopped sprinting
and I spent the night. There behind the weight
room, she stands next to me, checks my range
of motion, twirls my arms slow and watches
the shoulder rise and fall, lung and gasp.

She asks me to grasp my hands behind my back—
a feat neither my father nor I can perform.
"Your arc is perfect for javelin," she says.
She tapes my shin splints, first foam pre-wrap
to save the skin, "Like silk protects corn," she says.
She does not know Who Gets Kissed.

She lives near her parents' house now,
adopted a cat named Milo. She bends
at her upright piano the way she leaned

into my body, noting injury to muscle
and tendon. The way I almost bent
toward her. The way I always bend.

TRICIA ASKLAR

OLD ORCHARD

I learned how to coil a hose below the zoo's monkey
house in the eighties, wound it into wheel upon
wheel. The industrial-grade rubber, sage green,
the rapids spray out otter enclosure, guinea fowl,
elephant, red-ruffed lemur. Wendy throws it back
into rings, the same rhythm I try to mimic every
watering, correct my family, show them how
to swing out and in, each circumference a bible,
a long amble, the Sagamore just ahead if I squint.
She holds up jasper. She clerks evenings and endings.
Her rock glints. I cast out and layer. Every farm
wife invents her own arc.

TRICIA ASKLAR

DAY-OLD BREAD: FREE

"Still has some spring to it,"
the seller says as he pushes
in the sides of the oval, "you
can have it for free. I can't
sell it to you." I take the sour
dough he selects from six left
in the bushel basket, clasp
it and make for the traffic
light chirping. I feel luck
and a certain chalky beauty,
with my head of lettuce, kettle
corn and white paper chinked
between arm and torso. The
gallery is now a music shop
with a hundred guitars and one
accordion. I find a feather in a Ziploc
of kid's prizes, buy a messenger
bag for a dollar. I'm an undertaker
of unused or objectionable items.
I run my fingers over scarves,
buy wool products, sniff soaps,
stroke the bony dog who noses
my calf. We all seem bare
in the sunlight. We all could
use a handout.

TRICIA ASKLAR

DRY GROUND

JAYNE MOORE WALDROP

I stumble on a fragment of curb, nearly turning an ankle, as I cross a disintegrating asphalt slab, a remnant of the street where I once lived. Without conscious thought I glance in both directions, more from childhood habit than necessity. There are no cars left. There's nothing left, only a few shards of brick and stone, a faint curvature of sky and earth that feels vaguely familiar. I wander through this unmarked place, dead to me for forty years, remembering each house and family and tree that had been here before the water came.

It was an old town built along the Cumberland, that ancient channel snaking its way through the middle of the country from the mountains to the barrens and back to hills. The government said we needed flood control. Hydroelectric power. That we'd benefit from tourists in ski boats skimming along the giant lake that would rise when the river was dammed. They also said we had no choice.

Maybe some of the adults realized what we were losing when they moved us out—I was a kid, not privy to their conversations—but others jumped at the chance to leave this place and its floods, where the river crawled out of its bed and slipped into town at least once a year, usually in late winter or spring. People tired of pumping out wet basements, shoveling mud-caked streets and sidewalks, and moving furniture to the attic. The chance to live on higher ground lured them away, encouraged by the gift of free land for those who committed to build in the new town that sprouted in a cornfield two miles away.

■ ■ ■

"Our lot's on Dogwood Lane," my father said, holding a freshly inked deed in his hand. "Construction starts Monday, so we have to choose which model we want." His eyes were bright, his words spoken in a rush.

"That's a pretty name for a street," my mother said. "Have you seen the house plan book? We've got so much to decide."

The new town would be called Columbia, the developers announced, and they gave each homeowner a book to help them design their homes. The book's cover pictured a family dressed like they had been to church or a funeral, except they looked too happy to have come from a graveyard. The parents smiled: she wore a hat and pearl necklace, he was in suit and tie. The girl and boy looked like they would never fight or call each other names the way my sister Becky and I did. From a new car they walked toward a fine example of a modern home, the kind everyone wanted in 1963. I knew our family didn't look like those people or dress like them, even on Easter Sunday. Our clothes weren't as fancy and our car was old, but we were getting a new house.

In the house plan book were ten drawings by an architect from Fort Worth, Texas, who specialized in new subdivisions. Most were one-level styles, but there were other new types called split levels and bi-levels, with the choice of all brick, all siding, or somewhere in between. Next to the picture of the outside was another drawing, a series of lines that formed boxes of different sizes labeled LR, DR, KIT, BR, BA.

A new house in a new town sounded like a nice place to live.

"This is how the house will look on the inside," Mother said. "These are the rooms."

"That doesn't look like a house," I said. "It's flat."

"Pretend you're looking down, into the house, and it doesn't have a roof. Each line is a wall, and the walls make rooms."

She pushed her fingernail along the drawing to give me a tour of the house.

"You walk through the front door into the living room, and here's the picture window. This is the kitchen. Our table would go here. And down this hall is Becky's bedroom, and our room, and this would be your room." She pointed to a small box.

"I get my own room?"

"You sure do. Your room has a window, so you can see the street."

"What color is it?"

"Whatever you want, Cam."

A new house in a new town sounded like a nice place to live.

■ ■ ■

Three months later, we packed up everything at the old house, locked the front door, and headed to our new town, a place that was flat and dusty, with nothing to commend it but the fact it was beyond the reach of the water. It was the town of the future, not of the past.

Columbia filled with people from the old town. Everyone had been bought out, and most decided to come to the new town, but somehow we weren't the same people. We looked different in new buildings and on fresh sidewalks, seemingly familiar yet almost unrecognizable. We had new routines, shopped in different stores, and altered our boundaries. We couldn't see or smell the river each day. We no longer needed to worry if the water was high or low.

Our mother said the brand-new elementary school looked modern and cheerful. Inside, the floors were shiny, the desktops uncarved, and the seat bottoms not yet blemished with gum wads. The spines of the full-color third-grade textbooks crackled when we opened them for the first time. Outside, the sun felt hot when we played kickball at recess. There were no trees and the newly sown grass wore down under the treads of sneakers. Our old school, with its rows of swing sets on a playground shaded by giant oaks, was scheduled to be torn down before the lake waters rose. So were our old homes.

Neville Burgess, one of the boys in my class, came up to me during recess. I noticed how sweat rolled down his cheek from little sideburns his barber had created.

"Your house is next," he said.

"What's that mean?" I said.

"The bulldozers parked next to your old house yesterday."

"How do you know?"

"Rode my bike after school. I go every day."

"You're not supposed to be there."

"Those old bastards don't need to know everything," he said, defiantly. Neville liked to cuss; I guess he learned it from his dad. They lived three houses from our old place, and we used to hear his dad hollering during the summer when everybody's windows were open. That man could sure cuss, my mother once said. After the buyout and before the move, we heard him shout and cuss even more, and most of the bad words were aimed at the government and the U.S. Army Corps of Engineers. Mr. Burgess had held out for as long as he could. He was one of the last to sell.

"They might be tearing it down right this instant," Neville said. "They're moving down the old street and there's not much left. It'll all be gone by the end of the week."

"How far is it to get there?" I asked. I didn't have my bearings yet. The old town seemed like a million miles away.

"Not far, really. We'll go the back way so nobody sees us," he said. "The government owns it all now and they've put up fences, but I know how to get in." Neville looked less defiant now.

"I'll think about it," I said.

"If you want to see it before it's gone, meet me at the end of your street right after school. Change clothes, though. I'm not towing you on my bike if you're wearing a dress."

■ ■ ■

For the last hour of school, I thought about the old house. I'd heard my parents talk about people being arrested for going back to visit their land before it was flooded by the new lake. Trespassing, my dad had said. I'd heard the word in church so I knew it was something I wasn't supposed to do, but I couldn't recall my parents telling me to not go to the old town. I walked home from school, changed clothes, and said I was going to play baseball at school. Neville was waiting for me, like he said he would.

"Get on," he said. We took off down a dirt path through pastures and woods. We stayed away from the main road.

"You sure you know the way?"

"I've been going every afternoon since school started. I can find it."

We rode on. Neville stood up to pedal so I had most of the seat. I tried not to hold onto him or touch his blue plaid any more than necessary, but I couldn't help it when we bounced hard along the path. He pumped the pedals vigorously to make it up the last steep hill, but my extra weight made it impossible. We got off and walked the rest of the way to the top.

"Do you know where you are?" he asked.

"Not really. Nothing looks familiar."

"We're up on Pea Ridge," he said.

Pea Ridge was a limestone bluff that overlooked the entire valley and the river. A few old farmhouses on the ridge wouldn't be torn down because the lake level would never get this high. The cemetery didn't have to be moved either.

"But where is everything?" I said. I saw orangey red dirt and uprooted trees, churned and splintered, as if an angry giant, awakened by the ruckus, stepped down from the ridge to smash it all.

"This is all that's left, Cam," he said, pointing. "Looks like they took the roof off your house today."

"Where? I don't see it." I squinted to follow his finger but couldn't find our house. "Can we get closer?"

"We're not supposed to. The signs say stay out, but sometimes I walk around down there when nobody's working," he said.

We listened for sounds of workers or their machinery and heard none. Birds, singing like normal, were the only signs of life. We hid the bike behind a boulder and started walking down the road that led to town. The road was undamaged, still striped in yellow down the middle. Just past the "KEEP OUT" warning barricade, Neville pointed to a hill of red bricks that caused the chain-link fence to bulge.

"That was the shirt factory where my mama used to work," he said. "The front door used to be there." I remembered the large building and the whistle that used to blow at noon to signal the workers' lunchbreak.

We listened for sounds of workers or their machinery and heard none. Birds, singing like normal, were the only signs of life.

"Where'd they build the new factory?" I said. In my mind, everything from the old town resurrected somewhere in the new one.

"There's not going to be a new one. Those sonsabitches closed it for good," he said. "Mama's still looking for work." When Neville scowled, he looked just like his dad. Sounded like him, too.

We walked further into town. I saw a street sign I recognized.

"Water Street. Now I know where we are," I said. I looked to the left and spotted my old house.

"Come on, Neville," I shouted as I ran toward it. When I got closer, I saw that its windows and doors were missing, the walls jagged where its roof had been torn off. As we approached, bricks from the chimney fell into what had been the kitchen.

"We better not go in," he said. "It might fall down while we're inside."

I wanted to go upstairs to the bedroom I had shared with Becky, but I was too scared. Without the roof, the place seemed less like home and more like a drawing in the house plan book. I looked across the street.

"Miss LaClede's house looks fine. Let's go over there."

Miss LaClede, my piano teacher, had lived alone in the big white house built years ago by her grandparents. She was a very old woman, but she always served lemonade and oatmeal cookies after my lesson. We would sit in wicker rockers on her front porch, and she told me that she had never lived anywhere else. She was the last of the LaClede family, she said. They were all dead. Now she was, too. Mother said Miss LaClede didn't want to leave her house so she just died, right before they made her move.

We climbed the steep concrete steps that led to Miss Laclede's broad front porch. From here, the river looked wider than I'd ever seen it.

"Is the water coming up?" I asked. Neville nodded.

"That's why they're in a hurry to tear it all down."

From the outside, the house looked sturdy and untouched, but its neighbors lay in ruins, many smoldering from bonfires set to reduce the amount of demolition debris. Massive piles of brick and stone surrounded the house like the walls of a fort.

Inside Miss LaClede's, however, the process had begun. Pieces of the house were missing, like the stained glass window on the staircase landing. It once sparkled in yellow, green and pink in the afternoon sun, but now from the front hall, I looked through a hole all the way to blue sky. A carved fireplace mantel sat propped against the front wall, bronze chandeliers were stacked nearby, and the fancy wood banister had been ripped off the staircase. Miss LaClede was gone, and the last remaining evidence that she ever existed—her house—was being picked apart.

A small object on the staircase caught my eye. I climbed five or six steps, hugging the wall because the handrail was missing, and saw an old photograph. I picked it up and eased back down to the floor to study the picture. A boy, younger than me, his eyes closed, lying in a casket surrounded by flowers. The wallpaper and mantel looked familiar. I looked around Miss LaClede's front room. The dead boy had been here, in the very place where I stood.

I turned the photograph over and saw pencil writing so faint and curly I couldn't read it.

"Neville, where are you?"

"Chasing birds out of the kitchen," he yelled. "I guess they roost in here."

"Look what I found."

He walked into the room, carrying a broom.

I showed him the photograph.

"Creepy," he said. "Who's that?"

"Look on the back. Can you read it?"

He studied the old-fashioned cursive for a long time. "I think it says 'Francis, Brother, April 17, 1938.'"

"Is that Miss LaClede's brother?"

Neville shrugged. "How would I know? That was a long time ago." He stared at the photograph of the dead boy.

"Let's get out of here. I need to get home for supper," he said.

For a second, I considered putting the picture back on the stairs where I found it, but I slipped it into my pocket and kept it. I never showed it to anyone. Sometimes I'd take it from its hiding place in my closet and look at it, thinking of Miss Laclede. The picture of the dead boy was my connection to her, the only proof that she and her people had ever existed.

■ ■ ■

A few months after our bicycle trip to the old town, the lake reached its expected level. There are clues, if one knows where to look, that something used to be here. A slab of concrete or asphalt sticks tight to the earth where people once walked and cars used to roll. Jonquils bloom, every spring, next to the outline of a stone foundation. The incline that used to be Water Street, the hilly one that ended at the ferry landing, still strains my thighs.

Bulldozers tore down houses, stores, the old hotel where river travelers found shelter for more than a century, from Jenny Lind and the Marquis de Lafayette to officers of both the Confederacy and the Union on their way south. The land remains, somewhere, below a lake that advanced like an army that knew no boundaries. They said it was for flood control. They told us we'd have cheap hydroelectric power. That tourists would flock to use the giant lake for fishing and boating. All that was true, but they never told us how much we'd miss it, or for how long.

Decades later, my memories surface, unexpectedly, often in dreams, when I see the second-story bedroom I shared with my sister, its sheer dotted curtains fluttering with each pass of the oscillating fan. A towboat pushes a line of barges through twists of limestone and muddy water, and a whirling, grinding sound hangs in the air, partly from the boat's engines as it makes its way and partly from the kitchen below, where my mother whips cream and butter into steaming potatoes with a Sunbeam mixer. I watch the lake rise, slowly taking shape into the monster that swallowed it all.

I walk those sidewalks each night, wandering through an unmarked place, dead to us for forty years, remembering each house and family and tree. I dream of Francis LaClede, the swings on the playground, and tiny pearl buttons, scattered in the dirt where the shirt factory once stood. ■

FOR LACEY

What can I say about our dead cat
other than that we loved her
for nearly two decades?
That a friend and I would do our middle-school homework
sprawled on the living room floor with her beside us,
and I am thirty now.
That she was loud and welcoming
and eager to be held.
That her fur was a blanket.
That she stole bread and corn-on-the-cob as a kitten
and begged for ice cream and guacamole as a cat.
That I cradled her moth-soft head in my palm
as she died in my mother's arms,
that I kept cradling her head as her neck went limp.

JANNA LAYTON

BEE ON GLASS

I am inside,
drinking tea.
She is outside,
clinging to the window.
It is safe to admire
her yellow mink coat
and silk cape.

JANNA LAYTON

BOOK REVIEW

Fenton Johnson. *The Man Who Loved Birds*. Lexington, Ky.: University Press of Kentucky, 2016. 318 pages. Hardcover. $24.95.

Reviewed by Jayne Moore Waldrop

In *The Man Who Loved Birds*, Fenton Johnson returns to his native landscape in the Kentucky Knobs to revisit themes he has explored in past works—love, the law and the lawless, spirituality, solitude, nature. The novel is like a homecoming on many levels.

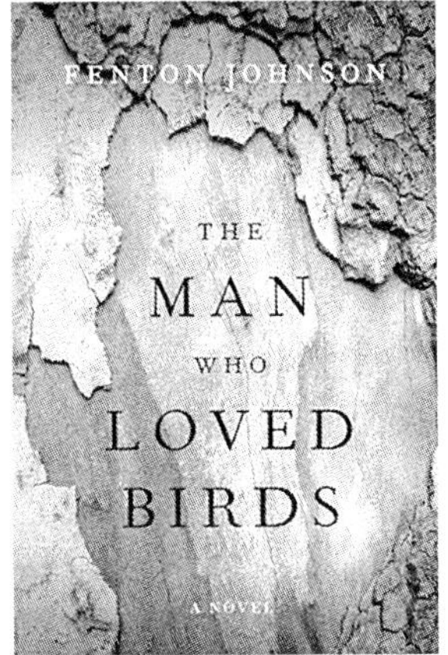

The book is a new release by the University Press of Kentucky, part of its Kentucky Voices series that began a decade ago as a collection showcasing the best of the commonwealth's literary traditions, including the works of Robert Penn Warren, George Ella Lyon, Frank X Walker and a handful of other acclaimed writers. Johnson's earlier novels, *Crossing the River* and *Scissors, Paper, Rock* have been reissued simultaneously as part of the series.

The Man Who Loved Birds is set in the 1980s, a period when the region around Nelson, Marion and Washington counties became the hub of the largest domestic marijuana-growing organization in the United States. The area received national attention when federal and state drug enforcement officers seized 182 tons of marijuana in an extensive sting operation in multiple states. In headlines and in legend, the homegrown marijuana cartel became known as the Cornbread Mafia. The bust sent many Kentuckians to prison to serve long, mandatory sentences under laws enacted during the Reagan administration's war on drugs. The novel includes a verbatim reproduction of a 1989 press release by the U.S. Attorney's Office in Louisville when sixty-eight people faced federal and state drug charges.

Johnson's research into the facts of the case began more than two decades ago when he wrote a feature-length article titled "High in the Hollows" for the *New York Times Magazine*, but inspiration for *The Man Who Loved Birds* began even earlier in Johnson's life. In 1971, he was a teenager in Nelson County, ready to head to California to attend Stanford University. A Marion County man known for growing pot and eluding conviction was killed in a suspicious shootout with Kentucky State Police. About the same time, a new doctor from Pakistan moved to Johnson's hometown. She was a Muslim woman who became the first doctor in years to practice medicine in the predominantly Roman Catholic community. The two events loomed large in Johnson's memory for forty years before he started writing the novel.

Three main characters form the heart of the story as they configure themselves into an unlikely triangle. Brother

Flavian is a Trappist monk who has begun to doubt his vows and ventures into the world beyond his central Kentucky monastery whenever he can. His character hooks the reader from the opening sentence:

> *Brother Flavian was not entirely certain what brought him, a Trappist monk soon to celebrate his seventeenth year in the monastery, to be standing in the Miracle Inn with a draft beer in one hand and a pool cue in the other.*

Dr. Meena Chatterjee is a Bengali-born physician who has been recruited to the area to set up a rural medical practice in a repurposed gas station. She is a skilled doctor but hesitates to take action that might jeopardize her immigration status.

Johnny Faye is a pot-growing Vietnam vet who uses outlying monastery land to cultivate his crop. He can't read and lives outside the law; he's also a storyteller, a bird lover, and the person that teaches lessons in transformational love to both Flavian and Meena.

The three share another bond through their connection to war: Flavian entered the monastery as a conscientious objector to the Vietnam War; Johnny's military service shifted his world view and introduced him to marijuana; Meena fled India after the war for Bangladesh liberation. Each leads a solitary existence, outsiders in their communities.

Johnson is a masterful writer about the natural world. His descriptions of the central Kentucky landscape are lush and recognizable. The woods, creeks, rocky soil, birds and snakes—particularly the snakes—come alive for the reader. Nature's rhythms are captured in lyrical passages that connect all living things:

This is the time of year in this part of the world when the glorious days of early summer lengthen and no one can entertain the notion that summer will ever end, that anyone or anything will ever die. Every living thing reaches to the sun, which is nearing its solstice but has not yet reached its brutal midsummer strength. The days are long and warm but the earth has not yet taken the heat as its own and the nights are deliciously moist and cool.

The author has constructed a world of sensual beauty, a landscape that feels both natural and mystical, made more powerful as a place that teeters between paradise and tragedy. Johnson's narrative is deeply rooted in the natural world in the tradition of Willa Cather, Reynolds Price, and Rick Bass.

The spiritual aspects of the story are likewise strong as it explores the redemptive power of love in a world of good, bad, and power-hungry individuals. The primary setting—a fictional Trappist monastery surrounded by the Kentucky Knobs—is automatically associated with the 150-year-old Abbey at Gethsemani in Nelson County. Johnson's childhood years were spent near the Abbey at Gethsemani; his family was well acquainted with the monks. He also lived in contemplative communities while writing *Keeping Faith: A Skeptic's Journey Among Christian and Buddhist Monks.*

The Man Who Loved Birds is a type of homecoming, a story about a place, its history and legends. The book's global perspective and unforgettable characters broaden its reach and keep it from feeling myopic or sentimental. And like most homecomings, it's a patchwork of memories, hope, heartbreak, and choices. ■

Crystal Wilkinson. *The Birds of Opulence*. Lexington, Ky.: University Press of Kentucky, 2016. 208 pages. Hardcover. $24.95.

Reviewed by Journey McAndrews

Crystal Wilkinson's new novel *The Birds of Opulence* opens with this passage: "Imagine a tree, a bird in the tree, the hills, the creek, a possum, the dog chasing the possum. Imagine yourself a woman who gathers stories in her apron."

Wilkinson then plaits together the stories of four generations of women who live in the bucolic southern black township of Opulence. Each woman in the Goode-Brown family has stories to tell, but her stories flow into the stories of the female kin who shaped and shadowed her. Together, these "lifetimes of stories are stacked up one on top of the other" until the women carry a piece of one another's herstory.

The novel centers on the lives of Minnie Mae Brown, family matriarch and great-grandmother, her daughter Granny Tookie, their daughter and granddaughter Lucy Goode-Brown, and great granddaughter Yolanda—whom Lucy gives birth to in a squash patch on the family's homestead early in the novel. Minnie Mae steadfastly tends to the homestead by keeping the ground hoed and the weeds at bay. The homestead is more than a piece of land tucked away in a holler; it is a place that binds all the women to their family's mountain culture.

Minnie Mae is a reader of signs and creator of remedies. Her neighbors seek her guidance through life's phases and stages—from weaning babies to treating colic, to studying nature and bodies, she has ways of knowing the world because she sees what others miss. On the day Yolanda is born, Minnie Mae is visited by a rare bird—"with a breast of red, freckled with gold," which she reads as a sign that her great-granddaughter will be born soon.

Joe Brown, Lucy's devoted husband and father of her two children (Yolanda and Kee Kee), is the only adult male allowed inside this female-centric world. Granny Tookie believes Joe is "a true, good thing," and indeed, despite feeling homesick for Ohio, and not understanding the mysteries and secrets afoot between the four generations of women he cherishes, Joe assumes the role of family caretaker and learns "how to blend into this river of crazy women."

Amid the sunlight and vibrancy of nature and life, gloom resides inside the Goode-Brown women. The women are susceptible to unhappiness and psychosis, or as Granny Tookie describes it, "The decent of old haunts." Gloom overtakes Lucy just moments after Yolanda is born—"a sorrow cloaked around her head that she couldn't shake." On the ride home from the family homestead after Yolanda's birth, the narrator observes, "A light summer wind picked up, whipped through the hickory at the end of the lane. The heavens grew dark, as if a storm was churning, but the sky blued up quickly and we traveled in the red blaze of the day's last sunshine." The storm is much more than just postpartum depression; what Lucy experiences is the thunderclap of mental illness that gives way to a tempest of sadness that exists within all the women in her family.

Wilkinson beautifully describes the physical landscape within the story's setting; with its verdant hills, sturdy silver maples, sunrise over the pines while the dew is still in, fog rising up like the hand of God, and endless wildlife. But she also portrays the psychological landscape created by a flock of wingless women who suffer from mental illness and harbor unspoken secrets. Opulence is a place where all is old and good, where every yesterday converges and is prone to shifting within the minds of the Goode-Brown women who are dogged by the memories that reach out, swirl around, and pound inside them. The collective hurts and haunts of these women resound throughout the novel like the sorrowful cooing of mourning doves.

Birds abound in the novel. Cawing crows, soaring buzzards, gloomy blackbirds, a barred owl, whip-poor-wills, a flock of sparrows, ducks, hummingbirds. Birds perch, flit, swoop and soar. Wilkinson utilizes the bird motif in ways that heighten the narrative. The movements of birds mirror the flights of depression the Goode-Brown women glide in and out of, and birds are an intrinsic part of Opulence's natural scenery. Birds also represent symbols and signs—good and bad, and they are metaphors for freedom and oppression, as exemplified through Yolanda, who wants to fly away from Opulence, while Tookie is as place bound as a mother hen—resigned to nesting for as long as it takes.

Minnie Mae, Tookie, Lucy, and Yolanda are free to roam the bountiful landscape surrounding them, and free to dream and imagine different lives and different places, yet they are caged by family dynamics. Although these women love fiercely, they clip one another's wings and peck away at one another's faults.

The Birds of Opulence is part of the Kentucky Voices Series at the University Press of Kentucky, and it arrives like "the grand whisper of daffodils in the spring" to mark Wilkinson's return to the new and noteworthy section of bookstores. It has been over fourteen years since Wilkinson published her first two books—*Blackberries, Blackberries* and *Water Street. The Birds of Opulence* is an important addition to Wilkinson's body of work. The novel openly addresses mental illness in a black community, is an exemplary example of literary fiction, showcases the author's captivating storytelling style, weaves memory and reflection impeccably, and invites readers to perch for a spell and keenly observe characters that seem oddly familiar, and astonishingly real.

Wilkinson writes so genuinely about the Goode-Brown family's experiences with memory, kinship, tenderness, anguish, hope, mental illness, laughter, care, and the desire to feel connected, that it is hard to think of them as mere characters in a novel. Their stories feel like our own; it is no wonder that they "greet us, like a hundred tongues whispering home, home, home." ■

Jonathan Corcoran. *The Rope Swing: Stories*. Morgantown, W. Va.: Vandalia Press, 2016. 144 pages. Softcover. $16.99.

Reviewed by Adam Booth

To the Outsider reader—the person who isn't quite sure how to pronounce "Appalachia" and perhaps can't locate its reaches on a map—the characters in Jonathan Corcoran's short story collection *The Rope Swing* will stand out as just that: standouts who don't fit the stereotypes of people who live in the mountains. The list includes old and young gay men, an educated female doctor who offers birthing alternatives, a young woman who is half Chinese, and the Appalachian expatriate. Because of this list, the short stories might appear as something different and remarkable. But those readers who know this area will immediately recognize most, if not all, of the characters in this collection; these people are a regular part of everyday life in contemporary Appalachia. What makes this collection noteworthy, then, is that these characters rarely get cast in the lead roles, especially within stories that are as persuasive and fully-formed as those Corcoran presents. Herein lies the beauty in his offering: the world of each story is crafted with a delicate but unabridged touch to the point that the reader can look past the novelty of characterization to deeply enjoy compelling storytelling.

While progressing through the book, the reader will find themes that connect these stories on several levels. Death factors prominently for both people and places. Corcoran's stories have an understanding that in the wake of older Appalachian industry and heyday, towns and once-great people will ultimately see their decline. "Appalachian Swan Song," the opening story, is a heavy looming decrescendo that bids farewell to the olden days of social structure in the little town that serves as home in most of the book. It approaches death as something inevitable, which can be difficult to witness in those people who were once the great figures of the town.

But the Appalachia of his tales also understands that someone or something must move forward, which reveals another major theme. Exploration of character is key to the success of most of these stories, and the reader can find satisfaction in seeing characters examine themselves and their relationships inwardly, forwardly, and back through time. This is beautifully demonstrated in the final two stories of the book, "Brooklyn, 4 a.m." and "A Touch," the only two that take place outside Appalachia. Here, the main character grapples with being a refugee, having left home and family to live sexually freely in the city. Those people and places which he most misses are the same that caused him to flee, creating a challenging pull against moving forward in life.

Another prominent theme is a strong connection to place. The small-town settings of many of these stories reflect the mountainous feeling of living on a land-locked island. The narratives show the complex reliance upon such a sense of place while simultaneously rejecting the social mores that have been established there. Corcoran's stories reflect the dichotomous feelings of Appalachian people who are The Other.

When I first read the collection, I found a major shortcoming with the eponymous story, the second in the set. In it, two teenage boys steal away to a remote area in search of sexual freedom to be who they know they are. The voice used in narrating this story was thin, two-dimensional, and at times verged on what you might expect in a romance novel. It wasn't until I was two-thirds of the way through the entire book that an element of craft revealed itself to me: each story is written with a tone that reflects its main character. This makes wonderful sense considering the collection represents the voices of those who are often overlooked in this genre of literature. When I reread the book, suddenly the title story didn't come across as being superficial. The second time, the narration read with the inexperience and sexual curiosity of a closeted seventeen-year-old young man. The story bloomed and the character's timidity found a sense of belonging among countless other isolated young Appalachians. I found a similar narrative satisfaction with other stories. In "Hank The King," the title character leads two lives. As a father, husband, and businessman, Hank is a triple failure. But the cause of his social defeats is in question: were those his doings or the products of a town in decline? Hank finds respite in his second life as a gambling addict bumming with colorful characters at the local American Legion. At times the narrative has a perfectly suitable lackluster impotence, at times the voice of an abused mutt, and at the moment of validation, that of a high school All-Star who returns to glory decades later. The familiar narrative of long-term issues with temporary fixes makes a solid allegorical point to greater Appalachian predicaments. Corcoran's narratives are spot-on and his skill for communicating tough situations is great.

Perhaps the deepest understanding of difficult human condition is revealed in "Felicitations," where an educated, independent female doctor returns home to serve a rural practice. With quickly-established sweeping character, we see the doctor—who normally guides women through alternatives to birth—suddenly forced into a familiar decision when the stonewalled life she built for herself gives way to an unexpected love.

This was not the only story in the collection that made me laugh aloud and cry before the last word was read. Indeed, the world and plight of each story is so real and relatable that on more than one occasion the glimpse offered in a single short story wasn't enough. I had to set the book down many times to breathe with the emotions and live with the inevitable realities. Because of this I'm eagerly anticipating a follow-up collection, hoping that Corcoran will freshly and genuinely reveal more characters and places that I've known all along. ■

CROWS' FEET

Watching the shallow pools
gather in the pockmarked expression
          of my weathered driveway,

I've seen the feather-jacketed finches
find a spluttering bath in the miniature wells.
          To see the hard-set

stubborn face stay, as though sleeping,
while little claws jig their way
          across it, still

warms the wrinkles
around my eyes.

IAN C. WILLIAMS

CONTRIBUTORS

Tricia Asklar's poems have appeared in *The Bakery, Big River Poetry Review, Boxcar Poetry Review, Cold Mountain Review, Juked, Neon, Poet Lore, Tupelo Quarterly, Verse Daily* and *Weave*. Recently, her work was selected for the anthologies *ARTLines2: Art Becomes Poetry* and *My Cruel Invention*. Asklar's full-length manuscript was a finalist for the 2015 Moon City Press Poetry Award. She lives with her wife and three kids near Boston and teaches writing at Stonehill College.

Stephanie Barton lives with her husband and dog in Albuquerque, where she works as a freelance editor. Her work appears or is forthcoming in *The Louisville Review, Under the Gum Tree*, and the anthology *Get Satisfied: How 20 People Like You Found the Satisfaction of Enough*. She has also written articles ForbesTraveler.com and Investopedia.com. Barton is completing a memoir about family racial tension, hoarding, and learning to love by leaving home.

Adam Booth is a young Appalachian storyteller and musician. Born and raised in West Virginia, the study of Appalachian history and culture lies at the heart of his award-winning work. His telling appearances include Teller-In-Residence at the International Storytelling Center, New Voice at the National Storytelling Festival, resident at the Banff Centre (Alberta) Spoken Word program, and multiple events in fifteen states.

Mary Grimm has a short story collection, *Stealing Time*, and a novel, *Left to Themselves*, published by Random House. Her stories have appeared in a number of magazines and journals, including *The New Yorker, The Journal, The Bellingham Review*, and *Hunger Mountain*. She teaches fiction writing and the graphic novel at Case Western Reserve University.

Silas House is the nationally bestselling author of six novels, most recently *Same Sun Here* (with Neela Vaswani), as well as three plays and one book of creative nonfiction. He is a frequent contributor to the *New York Times* and his writing has appeared in *Newsday, Oxford American, Narrative*, and many others. House serves as the NEH

Chair of Appalachian Studies at Berea College and on the fiction faculty at Spalding University's MFA in creative writing.

Rebecca Gayle Howell is the author of *Render/An Apocalypse*, which was selected by Nick Flynn for the Cleveland State University First Book Prize and was a 2014 finalist for *ForeWord Review*'s Book of the Year. Among her awards are fellowships from the Fine Arts Work Center in Provincetown and the Carson McCullers Center, as well as a 2014 Pushcart Prize. Native to Kentucky, Howell is the Poetry Editor at *Oxford American*.

Jeremy B. Jones is the author of the memoir *Bearwallow: A Personal History of a Mountain Homeland*, which won a Gold IPPY in the memoir category in 2015. Hist essays have appeared in *Oxford American*, *Brevity*, and *The Iowa Review*, among other publications, and he teaches creative writing at Western Carolina University.

Janna Layton is a writer and office worker trying to get by in San Francisco. Her poetry and fiction have been published in various literary journals, including *The Rag*, *Literary Bohemian*, *Up the Staircase Quarterly*, *Bartleby Snopes*, and *The Pinch*. She sporadically rambles on at readingwatchinglookingandstuff.blogspot.com.

M.E. MacFarland is from central Virginia. His poems have appeared or are forthcoming in *The Southern Review*, *Fugue*, *Iron Horse*, *Nimrod*, *Newfound*, *Letters*, and elsewhere. He received an MFA from the University of Virginia and lives in Charlottesville, where he is a business journalist by day.

Journey McAndrews is a poet and essayist who was born in the coalfields of Eastern Kentucky. Her work regularly appears in *Kentucky Monthly* and has appeared in *Kudzu*, *Motif*, *LILOPOH*, and *Inscape*. She lives in Lexington, Kentucky, and received her MFA in Creative Nonfiction from Spalding University. McAndrews teaches Feature Writing and Women & Gender Studies at Eastern Kentucky University, and just completed a food memoir, *I Eat My Peas with Honey*.

Jennifer Newhouse earned her MFA at the University of North Carolina at Greensboro. Her poems have appeared or are forthcoming in *Triquarterly, Lake Effect, The Chattahoochee Review, SAND, The Minnesota Review, Blue Lyra*, and elsewhere. She teaches creative writing at Chowan University and lives in Suffolk, Virginia.

Tim Poland lives and works in the New River Valley near the Blue Ridge Mountains in southwestern Virginia, where he is a professor of English at Radford University. He is the author of a novel, *The Safety of Deeper Water* (Vandalia Press/West Virginia University Press, 2009); *Escapee* (America House, 2001), a collection of short fiction; and *Other Stones, Kinder Temples* (Pudding House, 2008), a poetry chapbook.

Erik Reece is the author of *The Embattled Wilderness, An American Gospel* and *Lost Mountain: A Year in the Vanishing Wilderness,* and editor of *The Guy Davenport Reader*. His work has appeared in *Harper's, Orion, Oxford American,* the *New York Times*, and elsewhere. He has taught writing at the University of Kentucky since 1997.

Alan Teed was born and raised in Huntsville, Alabama, to a family that encouraged creativity and cherished photographs. He enjoys capturing honest images of the Southern United States. Teed now lives in Montana where he works as a wildland firefighter with the United States Forest Service.

Susan Tekulve is the author of *In the Garden of Stone*, winner of the 2012 South Carolina First Novel Award and a 2014 Gold IPPY Award. She's also published two short story collections: *Savage Pilgrims* and *My Mother's War Stories*. Her work has appeared in *Shenandoah, The Georgia Review, New Letters, The Louisville Review,* and *Puerto del Sol*. An Associate Professor of English, she teaches in the BFA and MFA in creative writing programs at Converse College.

Jayne Moore Waldrop is a Lexington writer and attorney. Her work has appeared or is forthcoming in *New Madrid Journal, Kudzu, Luna Station Quarterly, Deep South, Limestone Journal, Minerva Rising* ,and *Kentucky Monthly* magazine. A contributing columnist for the Louisville *Courier-Journal*, she writes a monthly column about Kentucky books and authors.

Ian C. Williams is a poet and the recipient of the 2014 Florence Kahn Memorial Award from the National Federation of State Poetry Societies for his chapbook, *House of Bones*. His work is forthcoming or published in *Blue Earth Review, The Altar Collective, Arsenic Lobster,* and other publications. He recently began an MFA in poetry at Oklahoma State University, though a part of him will always remain in West Virginia.